WORLD OF BRITANNIA

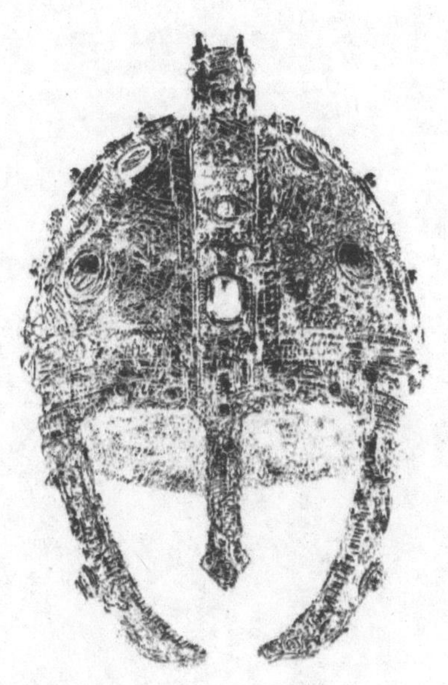

WORLD OF BRITANNIA

RICHARD DENHAM

&

M J TROW

www.blkdogpublishing.com

THIS SERIES IS DEDICATED TO TRISTAN

CURA DAT VICTORIAM

CONTENTS

THE *BRITANNIA* TRILOGY

BRITANNIA I: THE WALL

'Valentinian was shocked to receive the serious news that a concerted attack by the barbarians had reduced the province of Britain to the verge of ruin.'

Ammianus Marcellinus

The story opens in 367AD. Four soldiers – Justinus, Paternus, Leocadius and Vitalis – are out hunting for food supplies at an outpost of Hadrian's Wall, when the Wall comes under attack.

The four find their fort destroyed, their comrades killed and Paternus is unable to find his wife and son. As they run south to Eboracum, they realise that this is no ordinary border raid. Ranged against the Romans at the edge of the world are four different peoples and they have banded together under a mysterious leader who wears a silver mask and uses the name Valentinus – Man of Valentia – the turbulent area north of the Wall.

Faced with questions they are hard pressed to answer, Leocadius blurts out a story that makes the men Heroes of the Wall. Their lives change, not only when Valentinus begins his lethal sweep across Britannia but as soon as Leo's lie is out in the world, growing and changing as it goes.

BRITANNIA II: THE WATCHMEN

'Then [Maximus] sent a letter to the man who styled himself emperor in Rome. There was naught in that letter … but only this "If I come to Rome and if I come".'

The Dream of Macsen Wledig
Mabinogion

Britannia in the late fourth century is a wild, dark place and the *Pax Romana* that has held for three hundred years is crumbling. Our heroes of the Wall have moved on but once again find themselves facing a challenge that threatens to overthrow Rome itself.

The new name on everyone's lips is that of Magnus Maximus, one of the emperor's ablest generals. Celtic legend, Egyptian mysticism and gaelic battle fury are all interwoven in a mad quest for glory and undying fame. And how many of the Heroes will Maximus take with him?

BRITANNIA III: THE WARLORDS

'Britain was forever removed from the Roman name.'
Narratio de imperatoribus domus Valentinae et Theodosiane

In the twilight of Britannia, the Heroes of the Wall cling on to an ideal and to survival. The old ways have gone, the old loyalties are shaken. Nothing is certain any more and the emperor's throne itself is up for grabs. There are threats from across the German Sea as invaders circle the dying empire like wolves around their prey.

Richard Denham & M. J. Trow

HOW TO USE THIS BOOK

The *World of Britannia* is designed to accompany the *Britannia* trilogy and to provide useful historical background and related information.

You can of course read it from beginning to end and we hope you will, but it is a reference work too. Sections on people, places and institutions are clearly laid out; so that, for example, if you want to know what Mithraism was, you can find it in the contents and the relevant chapter. Maps, diagrams and a glossary are provided too.

Throughout, words printed in **bold** refer to the real people and places that feature in the *Britannia* series.

At the end of the paperback edition you will find blank pages for any notes or queries you may wish to make.

N.B. we would like to apologise in advance for any errors in basic Latin you may find in this book!

All maps and other artwork in this book are copyright M.J. Trow.

Richard Denham (Londinium) & M. J. Trow (Vectis)

TIMELINE

'The City to which the whole world fell has fallen. If Rome can
perish, what can be safe?'

St Jerome

If you went to school in the distant past i.e. before c.1970, you
would have been told by your History teacher that the Romans
under Julius Caesar invaded in 54BC and they all left in 410AD.
Neither of those dates is strictly accurate and, thanks largely to archaeology, (see HOW DO WE KNOW?) we now understand a
great deal more about Roman Britain than at any time since the
fifth century.

Briefly, the Romans believed they had a natural right to
conquer and colonise, turning a struggling little settlement on the
banks of the Tiber into the most powerful and organized empire in
the ancient world. Perhaps only the Mongol Empire of the thirteenth century and certainly the British Empire of the nineteenth
would be bigger. Today, Julius Caesar would be regarded as a war
criminal. He engineered a war against the Gauls (today's French-
men) and in defeating them, led two expeditions to the island the
Romans called Britannia in 55 and 54BC.

This was no more than a toe-hold and the 'real' permanent
Roman colonisation took place in 43AD under the Emperor Claudius. Again, this is the shorthand of history – the hard work of
conquest was actually carried out by generals like Aulus Plautius
and Vespasian; Claudius just turned up at the end to take the credit
– that was the way with emperors!

Over the next century, Britannia became a province of the empire, ruled from Rome and policed by the legions. Towns called coloniae grew up around legionary bases; straight, cobbled roads linked them. Rich men built expensive villas for themselves and out of an uneasy peace between the invaders and the locals, Roman Britain was forged.

There were setbacks for the Romans – local heroes emerged who fought them: Caratacus in what is Wales today; Boudicca, the flame-haired queen from Norfolk. In the far north, the wild tribes of what is today Scotland never surrendered to Roman rule and the legions never set foot in Ireland. Apart from the flash-points however, there was mutual trust based on trade and agriculture and the *Pax Romana* (the Roman Peace) became the norm.

Inevitably, because Britannia was just a tiny part of a vast empire that stretched from Pembrokeshire to Palmyra, political, economic and religious events happening elsewhere sometimes had an impact in this country too. The *Britannia* series covers the years 367-415AD and we hope the timeline below will be helpful.

The most famous Roman of them all. Julius Caesar landed on the south coast in 55BC, returning the following year with the first force to occupy Britannia. (Source: Museo Nationale, Naples)

The emperor Claudius from a bronze head found in the River Alde and probably from the temple at Camulodunum (Colchester). Note the Julius Caesar hairstyle worn by all emperors for four centuries. Claudius seems to be rather coy about his age; he was over fifty when he landed in Britannia in 43AD.

364   Valentinian is elected emperor by the army. He rules in the West, including Britannia. His younger brother Valens rules the East.

367   The Great Conspiracy in Britannia. For the first time, the Picts, Scots, Attacotti, Franks and local British tribes band together and attack Hadrian's Wall before raiding south.

Valentinian falls ill and names his nine-year-old son **Gratian** as his co-ruler (Augustus).

368   **Flavius Theodosius** is sent to Britannia to put down the Conspiracy.

He brings with him his son, the future **Emperor Theodosius** and the general **Magnus Maximus**.

370   With the Conspiracy destroyed and order restored, the **elder Theodosius** is promoted *magister equitus* (cavalry commander) and defeats the Alemanni (Germans) in Gaul.

372-4   The **elder Theodosius** puts down a Berber rebellion in North Africa.

374   **Theodosius the younger** defeats the Sarmatians in Dalmatia (today's Croatia).

375   **Gratian** succeeds as emperor in the West. His brother Valentinian II, aged four, is appointed co-emperor.

376   **Theodosius the elder** falls victim to a political plot in Carthage and is executed. The **younger Theodosius** is recalled by **Gratian** from semi-retirement and defeats the Sarmatians again.

379   **Theodosius the younger** is appointed co-emperor by **Gratian** to replace Valens, but falls ill. **Gratian** goes to his aid.

382   **Theodosius** concludes a treaty with the Goths in Thrace (today's Bulgaria) allowing them to settle in the empire in exchange for military service.

383   **Magnus Maximus**, left behind in Britannia after the Conspiracy, is elected by the legions and claims the Western empire for himself. He defeats **Gratian** in battle and

rules Gaul and Spain. **Gratian** is killed by his own troops.

Valentinian II succeeds **Gratian** as rightful ruler in the west. **Magnus Maximus** strips Britannia's legionary bases to fill his army, leaving Hadrian's Wall and the whole province vulnerable.

384   **Theodosius**, now called the Great, is busy fighting in the East and is forced to acknowledge **Maximus** as emperor in the West.

387   **Maximus** invades Italy. **Valentinian** runs to Greece.

388   **Maximus** is defeated in three battles by **Theodosius** leading an army of Goths, Huns and Alans. **Maximus** is killed at Aquileia, near today's Venice and **Valentinian** is restored.

390   **Theodosius**, overcome with remorse at the slaughter of 7000 civilians in Thessalonica, humbles himself before Bishop Ambrose and the Christian church.

390-92 Thrace is invaded by the Visigoths and Huns under **Alaric**, but he is beaten by **Flavius Stilicho**, a half-Vandal general who may have visited Britannia at this time.

393   **Theodosius** appoints his son **Honorius**, co-emperor.

395   **Theodosius** dies. **Honorius** is eleven, his brother **Arcadius** (emperor in the East) eighteen. **Stilicho** is appointed **Honorius'** guardian.

396   **Alaric**, feeling betrayed by **Stilicho**, goes to war with him and is defeated.

401   The Vandals cross into today's Austria and Switzerland. **Stilicho** is forced to grant concessions.

       Patrick, the son of a Roman official, is captured by pirates and sold as a slave in Ireland.

       Alaric invades Italy, marching on **Honorius** in Milan. **Stilicho** takes yet more troops from Britannia to stop him.

402   **Stilicho** defeats **Alaric** at Pollentia, in modern Piedmont, capturing his family.

403   **Stilicho** defeats **Alaric** a second time, near Verona.

405   Despite **Stilicho's** defeat of invading tribes, Vandals, Alans and Suebi cross the frozen Rhine and begin a migration which will destroy the Roman empire.

406   Much of Gaul is overrun by 'barbarians'.
Two usurpers are elected consecutively by the army in Britannia – **Marcus** followed by **Gratian**.

407   A third usurper turns up in Britannia – **Constantine**. He crosses to Gaul and Spain with an army made up of the last of the old Roman garrisons from Britannia.

408   **Stilicho** is assassinated and **Alaric** invades Italy again.

409   Romano-Britons rebel against **Constantine**.

410   Rome is sacked by **Alaric** eight centuries after it fell to the Gauls. The churches of St Peter and St Paul are spared.

411   The emperor **Honorius** tells the Britons they must defend themselves from now on. **Constantine** is defeated by the emperor.
Officially, Roman Britain is no more.

HOW THE WEST WAS RUN

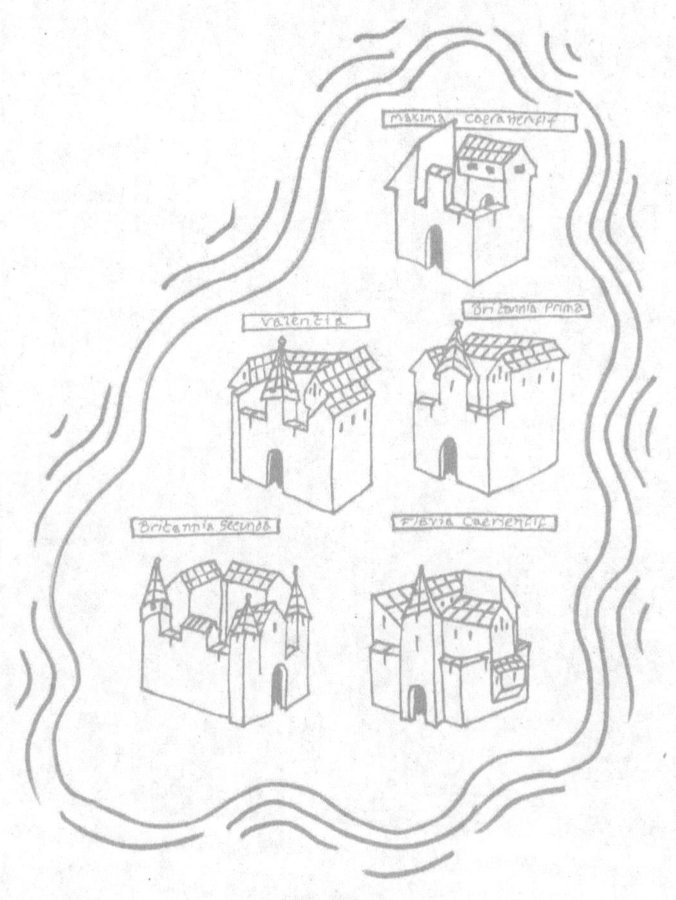

HOW THE WEST WAS RUN

Government and Organization

By the time of *Britannia*, the Roman empire was too huge to be ruled by one man. Constantine, who was declared emperor in **Eboracum** (York), had built a city on the Bosphorus, called Constantinople (today's Istanbul) after his death. The idea had already emerged of a co-rulership – an emperor of the West and an emperor of the East. Each of these used the title Augustus (the wise) and had a second-in-command, known as Caesar, after Octavius Caesar, the first emperor. The idea of four rulers, called the Tetrarchy, was set up in 293 by Diocletian and it was never likely to work well.

In practice the four ruled largely independently of each other, but bickering was constant over frontiers and who ran what. Under the emperors there were four Praetorian Prefectures, subdivided into fifteen dioceses and further sub-divided into 121 provinces! Grafted on to the system was nepotism. Constantine the Great left the empire to his three sons; **Theodosius the Great** to his two and so on. As Roman military power declined, emperors were increasingly forced to rely on leaders of alien tribes to augment the army – **Alaric the Goth** was one who would become powerful enough to sack Rome itself in 410.

We should not think of Rome as the 'eternal city' by the fourth century. Emperors moved their capitals, especially when an old one was threatened by invading armies, so **Alaric's** attack on

Rome was not quite the disaster we once thought. Even in the West, however, size was an issue and in the days when communication depended on the speed of a horse, it was essential that various officials below the emperor did their bit in terms of efficiency.

From a single province, which was part of the Prefecture of Gaul, Britannia grew into a diocese, a term used only by the church today and that was divided into four provinces: see Map 2.

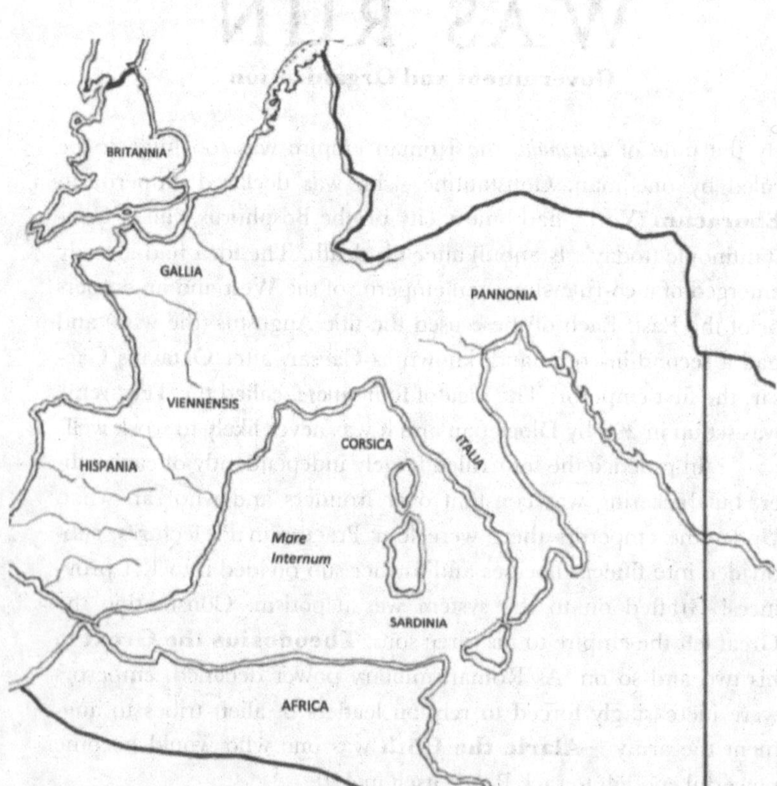

Map 1: *The Western Empire, c400AD. The vertical line on the right represents the frontier between the eastern and western parts of the empire.*

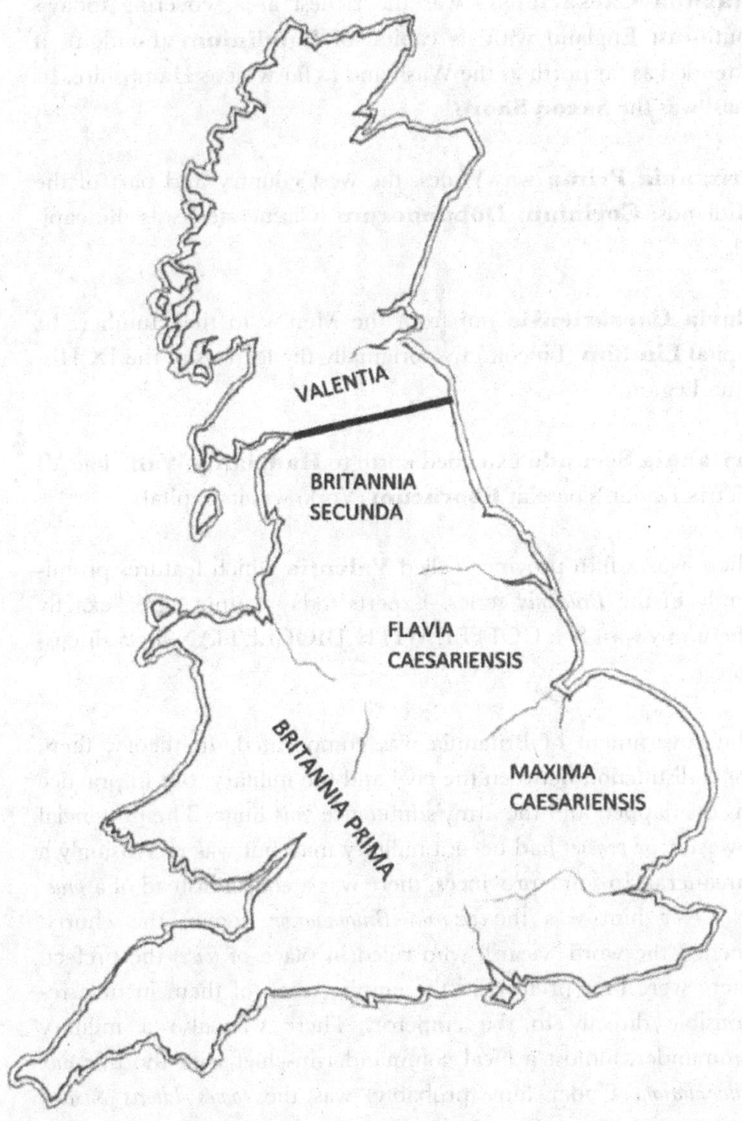

Map 2: *The diocese of Britannia showing the four provinces as they were in 400AD. Historians cannot decide exactly where the fifth province, Valentia, was. In the* Britannia *series, it is north of Hadrian's Wall.*

Maxima Caesariensis was the richest area, covering today's south-east England with its capital of **Londinium** (London). It extended as far north as the Wash and as far west as Hampshire. Its coast was the **Saxon Shore**.

Britannia Prima was Wales, the west country and part of the Midlands. **Corinium Dobunnorum** (Cirencester) was the capital.

Flavia Caesariensis ran from the Mersey to the Humber. Its capital **Lindum** (Lincoln) was originally the fortress of the IX Hispana Legion.

Britannia Secunda extended north to **Hadrian's Wall**. The VI Victrix Legion's base at **Eboracum** (York) was its capital.

There was a fifth province called **Valentia** which features prominently in the *Britannia* series. Experts today cannot agree exactly where this was. See COFFEE WITH DIOCLETIAN for a discussion.

The government of Britannia was complicated. In theory, there was a distinction between the civil and the military, but in practice this overlapped and the army's influence was huge. The provincial governor or *praeses* had been a military man but was increasingly a bureaucrat. In some provinces, there was a consul instead of a *praeses*. Over him was the *vicarius Britanniarum* (again, the church pinched the word 'vicar'!) who ruled in place of (*vice*) the prefect. There were four prefects in the empire, each of them in turn responsible directly to the emperor. There was also a military commander, almost a local commander-in-chief with the title *dux Britanniarum*. Under him (probably) was the *comes Litoris Saxonii* (Count of the Saxon Shore).

We can put names to these titles in the *Britannia* period:

Emperors
House of Valentinian

Valentinian I	364-375
Valens	364-378
Gratian	367-383
Valentinian II	375-392
Magnus Maximus	383-388

House of Theodosius

West   East

Theodosius I the Great 379-395

West		East	
Honorius	395-423	**Arcadius**	395-408
Marcus	406? (in Britain)	Theodosius II	408-450
Gratian	407 (in Britain)		
Constantine III	407-411		
Maximus	409-411		
Jovinus	411-412		

Vicarii of Britannia

Civilis	368
Victorinus,	probably 395-406
Chrysanthos	probably 395-406

There were also, at lower levels, pen-pushers who handled the daily minutiae of the provinces. These were called *decurions* and they were members of the *ordo* or *curia*, the rough equivalent of today's town and county councillors.

Please note how patchy the official record is for local government in the period covered by *Britannia*. The only other names we have are **Fullofaudes** who was dux Britanniarum in 367 and **Nectaridus**, Count of the Saxon Shore. The lack of information is infuriating – welcome to our world!

LOCATION, LOCATION, LOCATION

Richard Denham & M. J. Trow

LOCATION, LOCATION, LOCATION

Loci, Loci, Loci

'The home of men who are complete savages and lead a miserable existence because of the cold; and therefore, in my opinion, the northern limit of our inhabited world is to be placed there.'

Strabo (63BC-24AD)

Over a four-hundred-year period, the Romans built a great deal. Sadly for us, much of it has gone and we should be grateful for the survival of spectacular buildings elsewhere in the empire, such as the Pantheon in Rome, the Maison Carée in Nimes and Diocletian's Palace in Split, Croatia. Usually in towns, later generations pulled down or built over the Roman original, so that Aquae Sulis is now the Georgian spa town of Bath. In Winchester, the great capital of Alfred the Great has only a few feet of its Roman wall left. (See PLACES TO VISIT)

The good news is that new finds are turning up all the time, thanks to a renewed media interest in archaeology. Tiles, pottery and coins still litter the fields, feet below the surface and villas lie under the petunias in somebody's back garden. Modern archaeo-logical techniques mean that we now know a lot more about Roman Britain than at any time in history (see HOW DO WE KNOW?)

Below is an alphabetical list of places referred to in the *Britannia* series. The numerals alongside indicate in which book they can be found. Note that the Latin word *Castra*, a camp, has found its way into many modern place names, but they were not necessarily known by that name at the time.

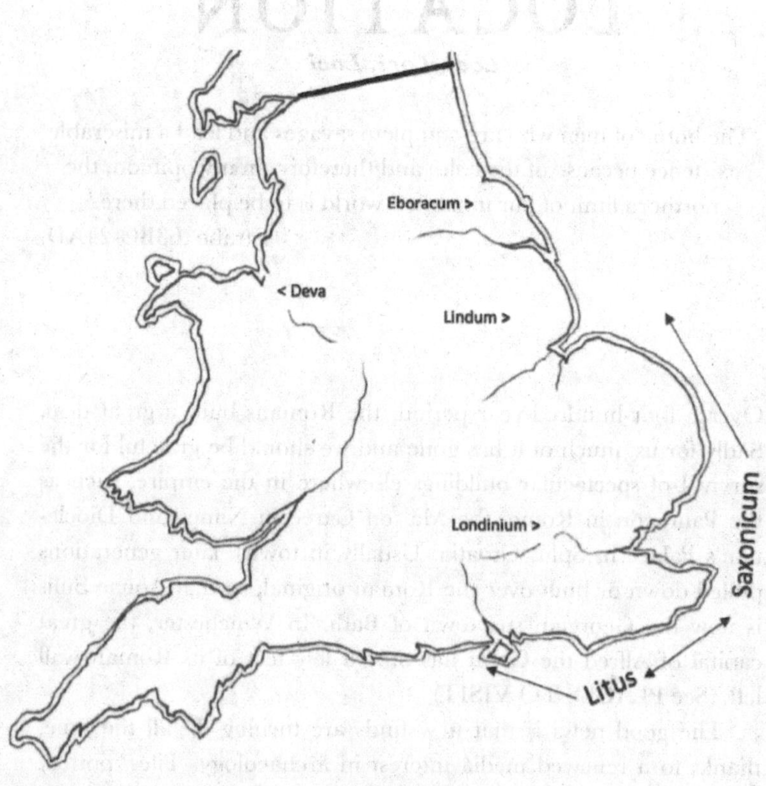

Map 3: *The legionary bases in Britannia, c400AD.*

Aesica (Greatchesters) I, II, III

Today, this fort on **Hadrian's Wall** north of Haltwhistle is overgrown and half-forgotten. In its heyday, it covered four acres. Excavations in 1894 uncovered the Aesica brooch, a superb example of fourth century jewellery now in Newcastle Museum.

Aldborough (See: Isurium Brigantium)

Anderida – also called Anderitum (Pevensey) III

A **Saxon Shore** fort built in the third century with an unusual oval shape (most Roman buildings were square or rectangular). The walls were probably twenty-five feet high and there were fifteen towers, of which ten can still be identified. There is a Norman castle within the old fort, the foundations of which used the original stone.

Anglesey (See: Mona)

Aquae Sulis (Bath) III

A health spa (the Romans were heavily into their mineral springs) in use throughout the *Britannia* period. Extensive excavations under the Georgian baths have revealed a complicated Roman lay-out with temples dedicated to **Sulis Minerva**. Her bronze head was discovered in the eighteenth century. Most famously, 1970s archaeological digs revealed a number of 'curse' tablets, written in bad Latin on lead alloy sheets. Typical is this example – 'Docimedis has lost two gloves and asks that the thief responsible should lose their minds and eyes in the goddess' temple.'

The head of a Corinthian column which once held up the roof of the baths at Aquae Sulis (Bath).

Arbeia (South Shields) I, III
A fort along **Hadrian's Wall** overlooking the Tyne covering over four acres. The granaries, *principia*, barracks and kilns are still above ground, a reminder that Arbeia was an important supply depot for third century campaigns further north. In the fourth century some of the garrison were Numerus Barcariorum Tigisiensa, boatmen from the river Tigris in today's Iraq. This is a reminder of trading links and the cosmopolitan nature of the Roman empire. Tombstones here are of Regia, a freeman of the Catuvellauni tribe from today's Hertfordshire and Victor who came from Mauretania in North Africa. There is an excellent modern reconstruction of the gateway, barracks and officers' quarters.

Augusta Treverorum (Trier) I, II
The capital of the Treveri, a Belgic tribe in today's Rhineland. The Roman settlement dates from the reign of Octavius Caesar (Augustus) and later boasted an amphitheatre and hippodrome (chariot racing circuit). It became the imperial headquarters during the *Britannia* period, with **Valentinian I** and **Theodosius the Great** living there. It was briefly the capital of **Magnus Maximus** and its famous Porta Negra (the black gate) is a second century fortification which still stands as a symbol of the city's power.

Banna (Bewcastle) I
An outpost of **Hadrian's Wall** six miles north of Birdoswald. There is evidence of building in the third and fourth centuries. Its runic inscriptions, Agnus Dei (Lamb of God) and depiction of Christ are seventh century.

Bath (See: Aquae Sulis)

Bewcastle (See: Banna)

Binchester (See: Vinovia)

Birdoswald (see: Camboglanna)

Bitterne (See: Clausentum)

Bowness-on-Solway (See: Maia)

Brocolitia (Carrawburgh) I
A fort along **Hadrian's Wall** dating from the second century. It is possible that the temple to **Mithras**, found in 1949, was destroyed by the Christians. The carvings from here (now in the University Museum, Newcastle) give us the best example of a Mithraeum in the country. There is also a well dedicated to the water-spirit **Coventina** which contained thousands of Roman votive offerings, mostly coins.

Caerleon (See: Isca)

Caernarfon (See: Segontium)

Caersws (see: Mediolanum)

Caesaromagus (Chelmsford) I, III
Perhaps the capital of the Trinovantes tribe, excavations here have revealed a mansio (a hotel for official travellers), a temple, shops and a bath house. Archaeological evidence shows that a serious fire destroyed the town in the late second century, but it was rebuilt and was still occupied at the time of *Britannia*.

Caledonia (Scotland) I, III
Today's Scotland was invaded by the Romans under the governor Agricola in the late 70s. There was a legionary fortress at Pinnata Castra (Inchtuthil in Tayside) and a string of lesser forts to the south. Agricola won a spectacular victory at Mons Graupius (perhaps today's Bennacline) in 84. At some time after this the Romans pulled out, either because the Highlands were too bleak or too troublesome or because they achieved no strategic advantage. **Hadrian's Wall** was built to mark a base line for the Caledonian

forts and a second, the Antonine (named after the governor Antoninus Pius) was set up twenty years later. By the time of *Britannia*, the Antonine wall had long been abandoned, leaving the country to the **Picts** and the **Scots**.

Calleva Atrebatum (Silchester) I, II

The tribal capital of the Atrebates covered 107 acres and the walls are the longest continual stretch in the country. Excavations in the mid-twentieth century revealed a complex town plan with streets in a grid pattern. The north and south gates still stand and there were two temples under the present church of St Mary, the original version of which may have been built in the *Britannia* period. The famous bronze eagle, not a legionary standard but part of a larger statue, is now on display in Reading Museum.

Camboglanna (Birdoswald) I

Camboglanna meant crooked bend. The five-acre site stands on high ground above the river Irthing west of Gilsland along **Hadrian's Wall**. The place was rebuilt several times and includes guardrooms and the commander's quarters. There is disagreement today over whether Birdoswald was called Camboglanna or **Banna**.

Camulodunum (Colchester) I

A colonia built under Claudius for veterans of the invasion of 43. The walls are still visible and there are traces of Roman tiles in the foundations of several buildings. The huge temple of Claudius stood on the site of the later Norman castle and the cellars here are Roman. When Boudicca, queen of the Iceni tribe, sacked the town in 60, the inhabitants hid and were massacred in the building. The bronze head of Claudius found in the river Alde nearby almost certainly came from this temple.

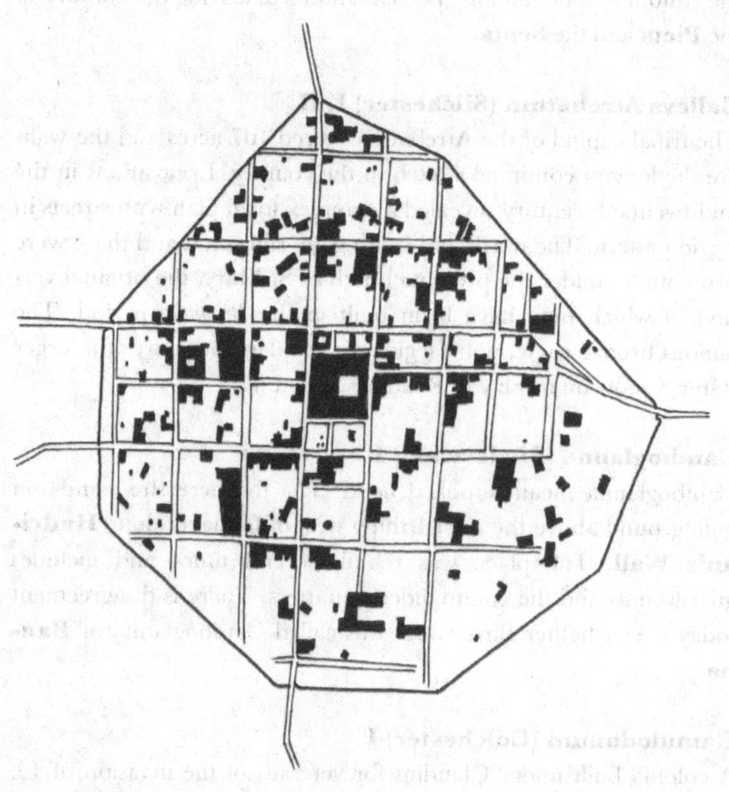

Town plan of Calleva Atrebatum (Silchester). The black shapes represent all excavated Roman buildings to date with the forum in the centre. The grid pattern was typical of all Roman towns as well as army camps and American colonists used the same idea 1600 years later. The Saxons did not!

There are excellent examples of Roman tombstones in the castle museum, including that of Favonius Facilis, centurion of the **XX Legion**. The most recent find (2004) is a hippodrome, the only one of its kind in Britain. It is currently a 'hot potato' between archaeologists/historians and town developers.

Caractonium (Catterick) III
A fort over the river Swale near Richmond, the town is mentioned by Ptolemy in his *Geographia* of c. 150. Unusually, it has retained its military associations and is still a garrison town today.

Carlisle (See: Luguvallium)

Carrawburgh (See: Brocolitia)

Catterick (See Caractonium)

Chelmsford (See: Caesaromagnus)

Chester (See: Deva)

Chesterholm (See: Vindolanda)

Clausentum (Bitterne) III
A port at the head of Southampton Water and the estuary of the river Itchen. It was strengthened as a fortress at the time of *Britannia* as Portus Adurni (Porchester) was abandoned. In the third century, coins were minted here with the letter 'C' (Clausentum) stamped on them. Part of the fort wall still survives. The Antonine Itinerary, a document listing places and roads all over the Roman Empire gives distances from here to Venta Belgarum (Winchester) and Noviomagus Reginorum (Chichester); today's Bitterne does not quite fit – welcome, once again, to our world!

Colchester (See: Camulodunum)

Corbridge (See: Corspitium)

Corspitium (Corbridge) I

A supply depot built by Agricola in the 80s and rebuilt under Antoninus. Most of the remains date from the fourth century. The granaries are among the best preserved in the country and there is a fountain and reservoir nearby. The legionary chapel is still there, where the standards were kept and five temples to different gods. The Corbridge Lion statue find was probably a fountain-fitting. The Corbridge Hoard, found in 1964, includes weapons, arrows, feathers and paper.

Derventio (Malton) I

A large fort built by Agricola that may have been a base for the IX Legion. Mosaics include the only British reference to a jeweller's shop. At some point the fort served as a base for Gallic auxiliary cavalry.

Deva (Chester) II, III

The headquarters of the **II Augusta** legion in **Cornovii** territory which was taken over by the **XX** later, there is not much left of the sixty acre site today. The Medieval walls follow the Roman originals and the town had the largest amphitheatre in the country, capable of seating 8000 spectators. Part of the quay is visible on the present racecourse and the Grosvenor Museum houses a superb collection of tombstones. The **Minerva** shrine is the only one in the country still in situ in its rock quarry.

Din Eidyn (Edinburgh) I, II, III

'Edin's Fort' dates as a settlement from about 8500 BC. The Iron Age settlements of the **Gododdin** were probably based on Castle Rock or Calton Hill, both prominent, defensive sites in the modern city and completely built over.

Din Paladyr (Traprain Law) I, II, III

A forty-acre site overlooking the Firth of Forth. It was an Iron Age hill fort occupied from around 1000BC and it may have been a burial place before that. It was one of the settlements of the **Go-doddin** tribe and the geographer Ptolemy calls it a 'curia' (house, in the sense of royal office). The name Traprain Law dates from the eighteenth century and means hill farm.

Archaeological digs in the early twentieth century revealed many layers of settlement as well as the famous silver hoard weighing in at 53lb. Some of this treasure probably came originally from Rome, **Ravenna** or even further east, from Constantinople (Istanbul). It may have been used to pay mercenary troops or to buy off the marauding **Picts, Scots** or **Saxons**.

Dorchester (See: Durnovaria)

Dover (See: Dubris)

Dubris (Dover) III
One of the **Saxon Shore** forts, not discovered until the late twentieth century because of the overlay of later generations. It was the headquarters of the **Classis Britannica** and tiles accordingly stamped CL. BR have been found there. The lower part of the lighthouse (*farum*) is Roman and it would once have been about eighty feet high. There was probably another on the opposite harbour entrance headland to guide the warships in.

Durnovaria (Dorchester) III
Tribal capital of the **Durotriges** built in the first century. There are two hypocausts, mosaics and a number of finds in the County Museum, including 22,000 third century coins discovered in 1936. The first inhabitants of the town probably moved here from the hill fort of Maiden Castle nearby. There was once an eight-mile aqueduct providing water for the town.

Eboracum (York) I, III (see TOWN ...)
The city was an important one in Roman Britain in the second century, the capital of Britannia Secunda. At first the legionary

base of the IX Hispana, it became the home of the **VI Victrix** after c. 120. The present walls follow the line of the Roman, with the Multiangular Tower its most impressive feature. The fortress covered fifty acres and the headquarters building (Principia) lies under the current York Minster. In the crypt museum here is the largest expanse of painted Roman walls in Britain. In St Sampson's square there are remains of the *caldarium* (hot room) and hypocaust (central heating system) of the legionary baths. The recent excavation and recreation of Jorvik, Viking York, uncovered an excellent Roman sewage system with tunnels three feet high. There are dozens of tombstones in the city's museums; evidence of a temple to Serapis, the Graeco-Egyptian god (yet to be found) and the huge carved head of Constantine the Great, elected to be emperor by the **VI Victrix** in 306.

Edinburgh (See: Din Eidyn)

Edirne (See: Hadrianopolis)

Glevum (Gloucester) I
A colonia (a settlement of retired soldiers) built in the 90s. Almost nothing of it remains but it was probably the home of the **XX Legion**. It housed one of the finest Roman tombs in the country, that of Rufus Sita, a Thracian auxiliary cavalryman. It was possibly once the provincial capital of Britannia Secunda (second century) and had expensive villas dotted around it. There is a modern statue to the emperor Nerva, traditionally the colonia's founder, in the town centre.

Gloucester (See: Glevum)

Greatchesters (See: Aesica)

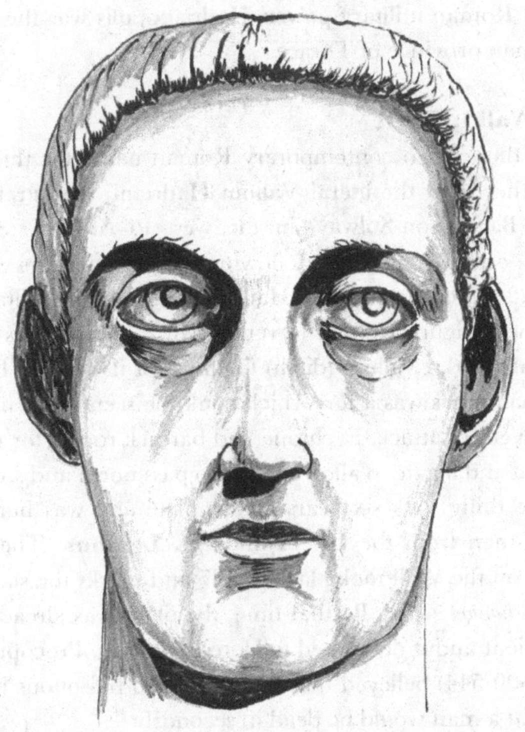

The emperor Constantine the Great who bwas declared emperor by the VI Legion at Eboracum (York) in 306. (From a bust in the Palazzo dei Conservatori, Rome))

Hadrianopolis (Edirne) III

The modern Turkish city now covers the Roman settlement of the emperor Hadrian and was the site of a major battle in 378 between the Romans under the eastern emperor Valens and Goths under Fritigern. Valens was killed and the defeat was seen as a symbol of the decline in Roman military power. Hadrianopolis was the capital of the Roman province of Thrace.

Hadrian's Wall I, II, III

Interestingly, there is no contemporary Roman name for this line of defence (other than the literal Vallum Hadriani) that stretched from **Maia** (Barrow-on-Solway) in the west to **Arbeia** (South Shields) in the east. It was begun following natural contours where possible, in 122 under the emperor Hadrian who came to Britannia that year. It was eighty Roman (seventy-two modern) miles long with stone walls and a vallum (ditch) for most of its length. Every seven and a half miles was a fort which could be seen by its neighbours in the event of attack. Each one had barrack rooms for up to thirty-two men and a gate to allow traders to pass north and south.

The whole thing took six years to complete and was built by about 10,000 men from the **II, VI** and **XX Legions**. The first serious attack on the Wall took place in 367 and marks the starting point of the *Britannia* series. By that time, the place was already regarded as ancient and it developed folklore of its own. Procopius of Caesarea (c. 500-544) believed that the air was so poisonous north of the Wall that a man would be dead in seconds!

Halton Chesters (See: Onnum)

Ilkley (See: Verbeia)

Isca (Caerleon) II, III

The legionary fortress of the **II Augusta** two miles from Newport, South Wales. The amphitheatre was excavated in the 1920s and was built at the same time as the Colosseum in Rome. It could seat 6000 spectators and was probably used for drill and ceremonial displays by the legion. The barracks, ovens and cookhouses of the **II** as well as a bath house were discovered in Prysg Field. One of the tombstones records the death of Julius Valens, a veteran of the **II** who died aged 100. Recent excavations have uncovered the foundations of a harbour and that the fort was still occupied into the *Britannia* era.

Isurium Brigantum (Aldborough) I

A town near Boroughbridge, fifteen miles from **Eboracum**, it had strong walls in the third and fourth century and may once have been a base for the IX Legion. Beautiful mosaic floors with animal designs and Romulus and Remus being suckled by the she-wolf were found in the eighteenth century. Two milestones stood there from the reign of the emperor Trajan Decius (249-51) and a bronze statue of a sleeping slave boy is in the British Museum.

Leicester (see: Ratae Coritanorum)

Litus Saxonicum (The Saxon Shore) I, II, III

The series of nine forts stretching from Branodunum (Brancaster) in Norfolk to Vectis (the Isle of Wight) has caused huge problems for historians. They were clearly important and some of them were newly built at the time of the *Britannia* series, implying an ever-increasing risk of invasion from Europe. They even had their own commander, the **Comes Litoris Saxonici,** Count of the Saxon Shore. It is not clear whether the name comes from the defences *against* the Saxons or whether there were already Saxon settlements along the east coast. The term is only used in the Notitia Dignitatum of the fourth century (see HOW DO WE KNOW?).

Londinium (London) I, II, III (See TOWN ...)

Whole books have been written on Roman London and recent discoveries, yet to be published, will make them all obsolete! The town was strategic because it was the lowest crossing point of the Thames and was something of a frontier town by the time it was sacked by Boudicca in 60. The governor's palace stood where

Cannon Street runs today and the basilica and forum lie under Leadenhall Street. There was a legionary fortress in the north-west angle of the walls which were extended and reinforced in the late fourth century by **Count Theodosius**. Stretches of the wall still stand and the foundations of the Tower of London show its south-easterly corner. A temple dedicated to **Mithras** was found in the Walbrook, a tributary of the Thames, in 1954. There are pavements, hypocausts and house foundations together with workshops and sections of the old river wharf. Much of this will be added to by recent archaeological work.

There was a bath house and amphitheatre at Cheapside and a number of gates in the wall can be traced to the period of *Britannia* – Ludgate and Newgate to the west and Bishopsgate to the north. Finds from all London sites reveal an extensive trade with the rest of the empire – amphorae for wine, salt fish, figs, grapes, dates, olives; glass and pottery from Gaul and Italy; millstones and yet more wine from Germany.

Reconstructions of **Theodosius'** walls show timber foundations driven into the mud (similar to the building system of Venice) with massive barbican or drum towers to defend gateways. The rough style of building indicates haste and perhaps even panic, to protect the city against a sudden surprise attack. The city which would become today's national capital was the capital of **Maxima Caesariensis** and was briefly called Augusta in **Theodosius'** time. Had the name stuck, today's Londoners would be called Augustans! Ten thousand small finds have been uncovered since 2013 in a 'digfest' that has seen the city described as the 'Pompeii of the north'.

London (See: Londinium)

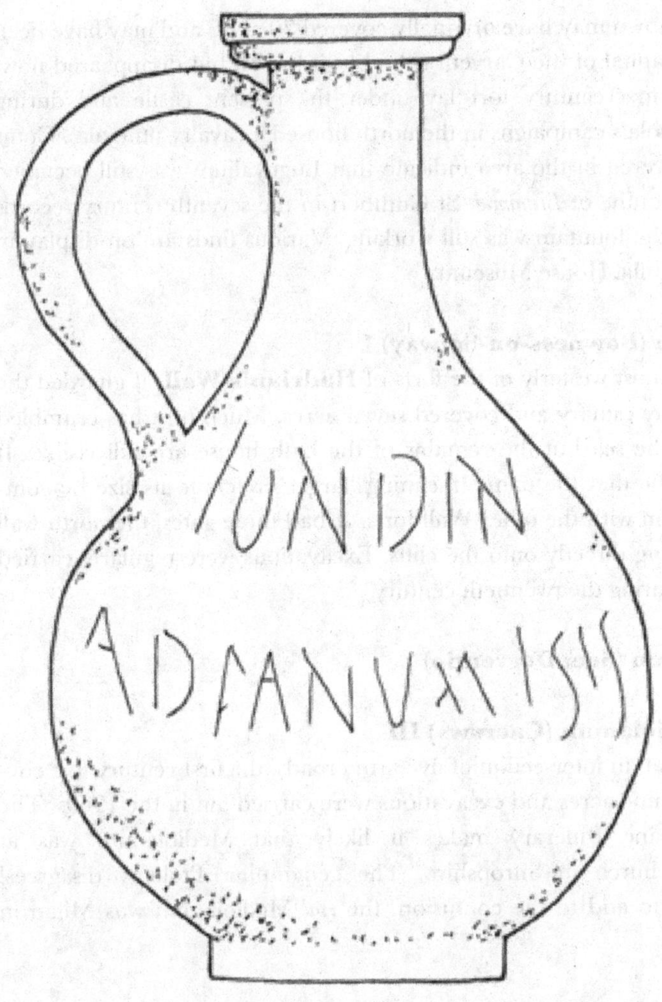

A pottery jug from the temple of Isis in Londinium (London). The inscription reads 'London at the shrine of Isis' Second century AD

Luguvalium (Carlisle) II

The town may have originally covered 70 acres and may have been the capital of the Carvetii tribe but it has all but disappeared now. The first century fort lay under the present castle and during Agricola's campaigns in the north housed a cavalry unit (ala). Coins uncovered in the area indicate that Luguvalium was still occupied at the time of *Britannia*. St Cuthbert in the seventh century records that the fountain was still working. Various finds are on display in the Tullie House Museum.

Maia (Bowness-on-Solway) I

The most westerly of the forts of **Hadrian's Wall,** it guarded the Solway estuary and covered seven acres. Much of it has crumbled into the sea but the remains of the bath house are still visible. It may be that the name (meaning 'larger') refers to its size by comparison with the other Wall forts. It had three gates, the north wall opening directly onto the cliffs. Excavations were regularly carried out during the twentieth century.

Malton (See: Derventio)

Mediolanum (Caersws) III

Built at an intersection of five army roads, the first century fort covered nine acres and excavations were carried out in the 1960s. The Antonine Itinerary makes it likely that Mediolanum was at Whitchurch in Shropshire. The geographer Ptolemy disagrees! And, to add to the confusion, the *real* Mediolanum was Milan in Italy!

Mona (Anglesey) II

The island off the north coast of Wales was the headquarters of the Druids, the Celtic priests written about by commentators from Julius Caesar to Tacitus. Their stronghold was attacked by Gaius Suetonius Paulus during Boudicca's rebellion in 60-61 and destroyed by Agricola in 78. There was a small three-walled Roman fort at what is now known as Caer Gybi which may have been new at the time of *Britannia*. If so, it was built to defend the island from Scots and Irish attack.

Newcastle upon Tyne (See: Pons Aelius)

Newstead (See: Trimontium)

Old Carlisle (See: Olenacum)

Old Sarum (See: Sorviodunum)

Olenacum (Old Carlisle) II
A fort on **Hadrian's Wall** which had a large vicus (civilian settlement) now only visible on aerial photographs. Some of the fort's ramparts are above ground on all four sides of a square.

Onnum (Halton Chesters) II, III
A fort on **Hadrian's Wall** north of Cambridge with an L-shaped layout. Part of the ramparts is still visible and the bath-house was impressive, with at least eleven rooms. Inscriptions tell us that the **VI Legion** built the place and in the third century, it was a cavalry base.

Pevensey (See: Anderida)

Pollentia (Pollenzo) III
An important military settlement on the road from Augusta Taurinova (Turin), it was the site, in 402, of an indecisive battle between **Stilicho** and **Alaric** which saw the Goths withdraw from Italy.

Pollenzo (See: Pollentia)

Pons Aelius (Newcastle upon Tyne) II
Named for the bridge that Publius Hadrianus built over the river Tyne, the fort stood at the original end of **Hadrian's Wall**, linked

to both **Segedunum** (Wallsend) and **Arbeia** (South Shields). Two altars there were dedicated to the sea gods Neptune and Oceanus and a number of votive offering coins have been discovered.

Pontes (Staines) II

A crossing place of the Thames since Aulus Plautius' invasion of 43. The name means bridges which probably tells us the Romans built the first ones there, linking the road between **Londinium** (London) and **Calleva Atrebatum** (Silchester).

Portus Abonae (Sea Mills) III

A Roman settlement at Avonmouth (now a suburb of Bristol) which may have been one of several bases of the **Classis Britannica**, the British fleet. Abona is the Latinised version of the Celtic name for river (as in Avon) and it is likely that much of the trade here was waterborne, especially to Venta Silurum (Caerwent) in South Wales.

Ratae Coritanorum (See Leicester) I

The tribal capital of the Coritani or Corieltavi, much of the original now lies under modern Leicester. The so-called Jewry Wall was part of the baths, built c 125. Magnificent mosaics were found here and are preserved in situ under the Old Central Station. A Roman cemetery was discovered in 2013 dating back to about 300 and there are examples of Pompeii-style scurrilous graffiti.

Ravenna (Ravenna) III

Made famous as the crossing point of the river Rubicon by Julius Caesar in 49BC, the town became a harbour port for the Classis Romana (the Roman fleet). Its impressive aqueduct was built by the emperor Trajan and in 402, **Honorius** transferred his capital here from Mediolanum (Milan). The place was difficult to attack, surrounded as it was by marshes and **Alaric** bypassed it on his way to sack Rome in 409-10.

Richborough (See: Rutupiae)

Rudchester (See: Vindovala)

Rutupiae (Richborough) I, III
One of the largest forts of the **Saxon Shore** built to defend the country's east coast, it featured heavily in Aulus Plautius' invasion in 43. By the time of *Britannia* it was a signal station, but its walls were massive and twenty feet high. There are triple ditches, stone shops and a *mansio*, the cellar of which survives. The fort had its own amphitheatre and baths. The latest defences, dating from the late third century, were probably made from timber. The principia was stone, as were the baths.

Saxon Shore (See: Litus Saxonicum)

Scotland (See: Caledonia)

Sea Mills (See: Portus Abonae)

Segedunum (Wallsend) I, II
A fort at the eastern end of **Hadrian's Wall** guarding the River Tyne. It extended to about four acres. The Notitia Dignitatum lists the fort as the base of the Fourth Cohort of the Lingones, from central Gaul.

Segontium (Caernarfon) II
An auxiliary fort guarding the Menai Straits between North Wales and **Mona** (Anglesey). Built by Agricola in the late 70s, it was still occupied at the time of *Britannia*. The *principia*, chapel and barrack block foundations are still visible and the Mithraeum was excavated in 1959. There are links in Welsh legend to Macsen Wledig, the usurper **Magnus Maximus** who features heavily in the *Britannia* series. Segontium was supposedly the home of **Elen Luyddog (Elen of the Armies)**.

Silchester (See: Calleva Atrebatum)

Sorviodunum (Old Sarum) III

An Iron Age hill fort which was probably a Roman posting station and lay in the territory of the **Atrebates** tribe. Only the ramparts now survive; the foundations on the site are of a Norman castle and cathedral, both later moved to nearby Salisbury. It is unlikely that the Roman army ever fully occupied it.

South Shields (See: Arbeia)

Staines (See: Pontes)

St Albans (See: Verulamium)

Traprain Law (See: Din Paladyr)

Trier (See: Augusta Treverorum)

Trinontium (Newstead) II

Even though this was one of the largest forts in Lowland Scotland, nothing of it survives above ground. Excavated in the early twentieth century, it contained altars which are now in the Museum of Antiquities in Edinburgh, a mansio of first century date and baths. A fine collection of armour was discovered here in an early twentieth century dig, relating to an auxiliary cavalry regiment from Gaul.

Verbeia (Ilkley) I

A small fort near the modern town centre, it took its name from a Celtic goddess of the same name, possibly connected with the nearby river Wharfe. In the second century it may have been the home of the Lingones, an auxiliary unit from central Gaul.

Verulamium (St Albans) I, III

The third largest city in Britannia, it covered over 200 acres across the Ver valley and stands on the line of Watling Street, the legionary road from **Londinium** to the north-west. Excavated extensively in the mid-twentieth century, superb mosaics have come to light, as well as the foundations of the basilica and the best preserved theatre in the country. By the time of *Britannia*, this was the town's rubbish dump. The whole town was badly burned during Boudicca's rebellion in 60, but the walls, shops and workshops can still be identified from before her time and Verulamiam's subsequent rebuilding. The modern name of St Albans refers to a third century Romano-Briton martyred for his Christian beliefs.

Vindolanda (Chesterholm) II, III

A fort along **Hadrian's Wall** excavated in the 1930s. There was a large vicus here, a civilian settlement of camp followers to the south. The towers have been reconstructed to give an impression of the original buildings, complete with a turf wall (*vallum*) and milecastle gateway. There were Gallic auxiliaries stationed here in the third century. Writing tablets were found which are unique to Britain, preserved by the chemical composition of the area's soil and a set of loaded dice, proving that dodgy squaddies have always been with us! The writings are a fascinating glimpse into everyday life, including a birthday party invitation, an order for socks and underwear and soldiers' requests for more beer. Bizarrely, the skeleton of a little girl was found here in 2010. She was about ten, buried in a shallow grave and had almost certainly been murdered.

Vindovala (Rudchester) II

A fort along **Hadrian's Wall** which covered four and a half acres. Five altars to Mithras were found here in the mid-nineteenth century excavations and there are specific links to the **VI Legion**. At the time of *Britannia* it probably housed auxiliary troops from Lower Germany, having been rebuilt several times after fires.

Vinovia (Binchester) I

A cavalry fort north of Bishop Auckland, built by Agricola, abandoned, then reoccupied c 160. The hypocaust is still there with an inscription *Numerius Concarigiensium*, referring to the foreign irregulars who often made up cavalry units (*alae*). Brand new archaeological reports of a six-year long dig are awaited.

Viroconium (Wroxeter) II, III

The town was originally a base for the XIV Legion, later the **XX**, but when the army moved to **Deva** (Chester) it became a civilian settlement. It was the tribal capital of the Cornovii, the fourth largest town in the country. A large section of the walls – the 'Old Work' – still stands and it once had an open-air pool not unlike modern swimming baths. There is an excellent reconstruction of a town house on the site.

Wallsend (See: Segedunum)

Wroxeter (See: Viroconium)

York (See: Eboracum)

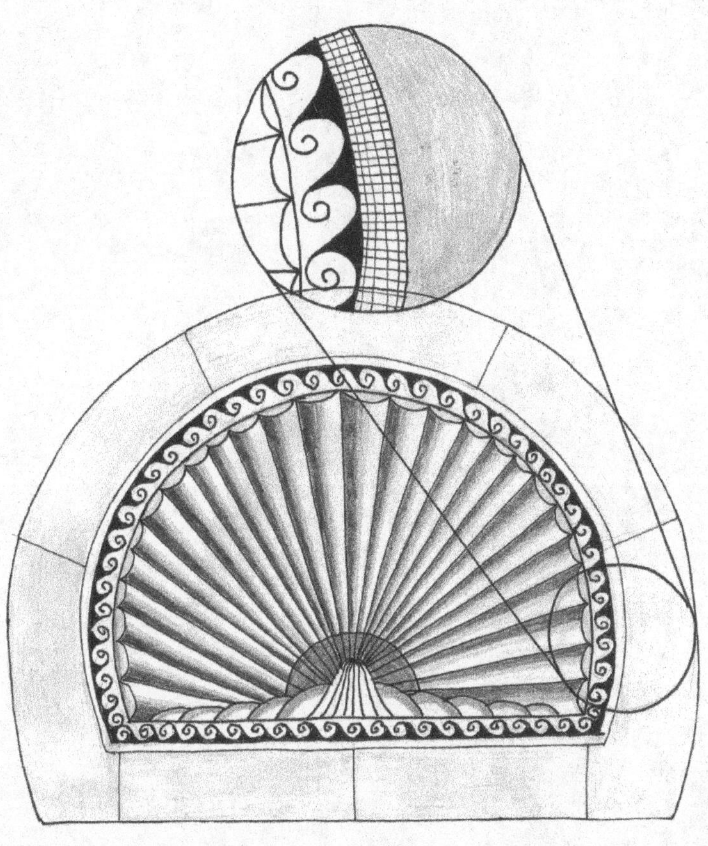

Shell mosaic from a town house in Verulamium (St Albans). The inset shows the detail. There are over 400 tesserae (individual pieces) in the section of the border as shown.

TOWN...

TOWN...

'The Britons were gradually led on to the amenities that make vice agreeable – arcades, baths and sumptuous banquets. They spoke of such novelties as "civilization", when really they were only a feature of enslavement.'

Agricola, 21

Archaeologists and historians have been wrestling for decades over exactly what a town is and how it differs from a village or a city. From our point of view, towns were a Roman invention, built where possible on a rectangular grid formation, depending on the lie of the land. Some of these were built over or close to an existing native settlement, usually referred to in the contemporary record as *oppidum*.

Broadly speaking, there were three types of town in Roman Britain: the colonia; the municipium; and the vicus. A dictionary definition gives us the basic differences between them.

- A colonia was a settlement of veterans, ex-soldiers who were granted land in lieu of a cash pension. **Camulodunum** (Colchester) was the colonia of the men who had fought under Aulus Plautius in the invasion of 43. **Nervia Glevensium** (Gloucester) was for veterans of the **II Augusta**. **Lindum** (Lincoln) was the 'retirement home' of the IX Hispana.
- A municipium had a higher status in a civilian sense; it was the forerunner of the Saxon burgh

which in itself often developed into a county town. It would usually have a charter issued by the emperor, outlining its rights and duties.

- A vicus originally meant a quarter or section of a city (*urbs*) and in that sense was not much more than a village. These were built and developed for economic reasons and never enjoyed the same status as the other two.

Eleven towns across the diocese of Britannia were civitas capitals, that is the 'headquarters' of a tribe, where the local civilian chieftain was allowed to rule as long as he broadly followed Roman guidelines. The original names of today's towns are a reminder of the tribe on whose lands they lay. Venta Belgarum (Winchester) was the marketplace of the Belgae; Venta Icenorum (Norwich) the capital of the Iceni and so on. Most of the towns of whatever type were fortified with walls, ramparts and ditches and had garrisons of *limitanei* troops. They were linked, for military purposes, by the straight roads of the legions so that military bases could send units quickly from one place to another. Interestingly, bearing in mind the importance of these roads, their original names have been lost. Ermine Street and Akeman Street are later names; the term 'street' is Saxon. Only the Fosse Way has something of its original Latin – *Fossa Via* means the way of the ditch. Very little of the first roads has survived; there is a one mile section of the original cobbled surface in Goathland in Yorkshire, known today as Wade's Causeway.

Even though Roman towns were built according to a common plan, which is, of course, found all over the empire, once built, they developed in their own way and by the time of *Britannia* the rigid grid pattern of streets had probably given way to a more haphazard and ramshackle construction in which there is very little evidence of town planning at all.

Then, as now, towns were the centre of business, administration, education and entertainment. For Roman soldiers and politicians, the country was somewhere to retire to; careers were forged in towns. They were run, as we have seen (HOW THE WEST WAS RUN) by the *ordo* or *curia*, the great and the good of the town, the members of which had to be thirty years old, relatively rich and exclusively male. In watered-down versions of Rome itself, individual *decuriones* were responsible for markets, tax collection, drainage and water supply, burials, the games, the law courts, the streets. In larger coloniae, there were probably finance officers, the equivalent of town treasurers today. The ordo met and carried out its administration from the basilica, itself built next to the forum or central market place. Public meetings were held here and probably court cases too.

The major towns had the baths, at once a place for relaxation and the hammering out of deals, economic and political. The best preserved today are at Bath itself (Aquae Sulis) but remains have been found everywhere, even in small army camps. They are usually put forward as evidence of the Roman obsession with hygiene, but recent toxicological analysis has shown that they were in fact centres of water-borne disease. The baths are certainly evidence of Romanization however and the fact that fewer of them existed in the *Britannia* period means that the Romans were beginning to lose their grip on the country long before the legions left. Some towns utilized the bath water by building aqueducts and street conduits that provided water for shops and households, as at Cirencester and Lincoln.

The houses of the well-to-do in these towns were comfortable but pale imitations of their Roman originals. They had separate function rooms, for dining, entertaining and so on and usually a servants' wing. But few of them had hypocausts, under-floor heating, and most were timber-built with wattle and daub in-fill. By the time of *Britannia*, brick and stone were widely used and the houses' public rooms at least had mosaic flooring.

Entertainment laid on in Britannia's towns cut across class boundaries. Amphitheatres, such as the ones at Verulamium, York and Leicester could seat hundreds of spectators and the Roman year, even in the provinces, was dotted with holy days in which gladiatorial displays were hugely popular. They were also expensive and it may be that most townsfolk had to put up with inferior shows of animal-baiting rather as many of today's provincial theatres cannot compare with West End productions. By the time of *Britannia*, there was a Christian aversion to gladiatorial combat (although judging by today's football crowds, there would probably be huge support if it were brought back!) and the games' decline is another example of the crumbling nature of the empire. Actual plays were performed on smaller stages and only three examples have been found in Britain – Colchester, Verulamium and Canterbury. Still rarer in this country were circuses, chariot-racing courses. The only one positively identified is at Colchester (see **PLACES TO VISIT**) and various mosaic depictions of charioteers is unhelpful as it may refer to events and people elsewhere in the empire.

Theatrical masks like this one were copied from Greek originals and were often held in front of actors' faces as in the Japanese Noh tradition. They were stock characters as in modern pantomime; this one is Senex, the old man.

The growth of a town depended on its economic wealth and this was hugely variable. Lincoln and Gloucester were both coloniae but the former doubled in size while the latter barely grew at all. It was all about the richness of the area (see … AND COUNTRY), the proximity of rivers and ports and, to an extent, the abundance of raw materials such as timber and iron ore. Permanent shops of all kinds have been discovered at Colchester, London, Cirencester, Leicester and Verulamium, many grouped around the forum. There may have been a degree of local specialisation which continued through history to relatively recent times. Cirencester had a market hall (*marcellum*) part of which was clearly a meat market because of the number of animal bones found there. Similarly, leather workers, linen workers and metalsmiths would tend to congregate together. Some shops were the 'front rooms' of domestic houses, open to the street and the family literally lived over them. Shopkeepers themselves were either outright owners, freedman-tenants or slave-managers. Goods were manufactured on the premises or at least locally and sold over the next few days. Archaeologists have been able to identify pottery and glass manufactories in Colchester, a coppersmith's at Catterick and London and a silversmith at Silchester. Wine merchants were everywhere, for example at Lincoln and York and stonemasons in all the towns provided building materials and gravestones.

In the service industries, fullers treated linen and wool and washed and dried laundry. There were eating-houses specialising in oysters (then a cheap, working class dish) like that found at Caerwent in South Wales. At Verulamium, one shopkeeper built a series of toilets for his customers!

To understand what towns were like in the specific period of *Britannia*, we will concentrate on the two towns that feature most prominently in the series – London and York. Both became major cities and important religious centres, one of course going on to become the national capital and today, the financial capital of the world.

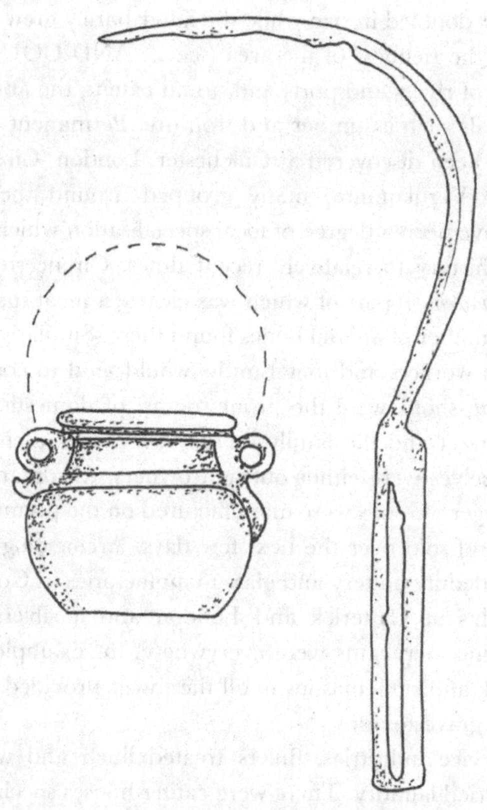

Strigil and oil pot from the baths in Londinium (London). The Romans did not use soap but instead soaked away grime in hot baths and slaves used the strigil to scrape away sweat and shed skin cells. The oil was used to moisturise. Roman men had body hair removed with tweezers — the screams could apparently be heard streets away! (Museum of London)

Londinium Augusta

The site north of the Thames was chosen because it was defensible and had a good water supply – the Thames itself and the Walbrook that runs through today's Cheapside. In fact, there were a number of tributaries – London's 'lost rivers' – that provided the future capital with plenty of drinking water and supplies of fish. The ground to the south of the Thames, today's Southwark, was much marshier by contrast and, as a result, building there was limited by comparison with London proper. There was probably no permanent bridge between the two until around 50 and it remained the only one until the eighteenth century.

It was still a largely wooden, 'frontier' town when it was badly burned by Boudicca's Iceni in 60, intent on wiping out as much of the Roman occupation as they could. Forty years later, under the just rule of the *procurator* Julius Alpinus Classicianus, the place had literally risen from the ashes. A new waterfront had wharves for sea-going merchant ships and a basilica and forum had been built on the high ground to the east of the Walbrook. There was an amphitheatre to the west and a garrison fort of eleven acres beyond that. The *procurator*'s palace stood between the Walbrook and the street that led straight from the river to the forum. Bath houses from the second century have been found both in Cheapside and Upper Thames Street, reflecting the complete Romanization of the town.

There is archaeological evidence of economic fluctuations in London which are difficult to explain. In the middle of the second century, under the emperors Antoninus Pius and Marcus Aurelius, workshops and houses were demolished; so were the baths. The implication was that there was a huge drop in population but its cause is unknown. It was still the largest town in Britannia however and its fortifications were improved. By the year 200, a two-mile-long wall encircled London, from just east of the Fleet River to the present site of the Tower. In places, it was nine feet thick. Five gates date from this period, their names still part of the modern city's topography: Ludgate; Newgate; Cripplegate (nearest to the fort); Bishopsgate and Aldgate. It may be that these sizeable defences were built in connection with the usurpation of the governor, Clodius Albinus, who declared himself emperor in 193 in a foretaste of the events in the *Britannia* series. By this time, too, Londinium was the capital of Britannia Superior (Upper Britain, though geographically in the south) and by the middle of the third century, an extensive building programme spread across the Walbrook and included new baths at Billingsgate and a large temple to Mithras (see SO MANY GODS). For the first time, a mint was established, under Carausius in 288, and it continued to produce coinage from time to time until the fourth century.

Under Diocletian's reforms in the early fourth century, London shrank again, if only because the two provinces of the diocese now became four and the town was the capital of Maxima Caesariensis.

By 314 London had its own bishop, who attended the Council at Arelate (Arles) in that year. From now on, Roman civic buildings in a variety of towns were appropriated for church use, to the extent that basilica, diocese and vicar (*vicarius*) have become ecclesiastical terms. A large fourth century building was discovered in 1995 on Tower Hill, which was similar in shape to St Ambrose cathedral in Milan. It may be that this was the original of St Paul's. There were a number of Christian attacks on the Mithraeum until it was finally abandoned in the middle of the fourth century.

By the time of *Britannia*, the public buildings of Londinium would have been tile-roofed and ragstone walled. The basilica that was demolished about 300 had been 164 yards long, the biggest north of the Alps. The 'locals' were anything but, with inhabitants from Gaul, Greece and Germany, with their own predilections for imports and foodstuffs. Olive oil, wine, grapes, figs, dates and salted fish were in demand and traces of all of them have been found in excavations. Samian ware, the red pottery so popular all over the Roman world, came from Gaul; lamps and glass from Italy. Millstones, pottery and probably furs were imported from Germany and the ubiquitous *garum* (fish sauce) was usually Spanish. There were bakeries around today's Fenchurch Street, although many homes would have baked their own bread. Steelyards and scales have been found which were used in calculating some of the weights and measures explained elsewhere in this book (see FRAGMENTI ET ROBERTI).

The outbreak of the Great Conspiracy of 367 brought yet more changes to Londinium. By now, it was officially Londinium Augusta, although the new name seems never to have properly caught on. The fact that **Count Theodosius** felt obliged to strengthen the town defences is testimony to the shock caused by 367. The original attacks were in the north, along **Hadrian's Wall**, but the rebels were many and mobile and could, in theory, strike anywhere. Archaeology has shown that the building of the walls in the late fourth century was haphazard, with the use of old stone rammed into clay foundations. The walls had timber foundations reinforced from inside by a chalk bank. There were towers at regular intervals which could house ballistae and be held even if the adjacent wall was overrun. All the town gates had circular-fronted drum towers on each side, a style of fortification that would continue into the era of castle-building.

In 429 when Germanus, the Bishop of Auxerre, visited Britannia, he found that the Roman way of life was still being carried on, at least in the south-east, although Londinium may have been shrinking again at the time. This was twenty years after the legions had left.

Eboracum

Eboracum was a colonia built on the banks of the River Ouse in Yorkshire. The river, like the Thames, provided fish and water, this time for the veterans of the **VI Victrix legion**. It served as a base for Severus and Carracala against the Caledonian tribes in the early third century and became the capital of the new province of Britannia Inferior (Lower Britain, though geographically in the north) under the command of a praetorian governor or *praeses*. It is possible that the large building discovered by archaeologists in 1929 under Old Station Yard in the modern city was his palace.

The legionary fortress under the Medieval Minster extended from today's Monk Bar nearly to the river but south of it stood an older settlement, the canabae, a collection of civilian huts and linking streets that were the equivalent of the shanty hovels that sprang up outside the walls of Medieval castles. In the late third and early fourth centuries, Eboracum had greatness thrust upon it because the emperor Severus lived there for three years. Constantius I died there and Constantine was proclaimed emperor by the **VI** in 306. Because of that it is possible that an imperial palace – a *domus Palatina* – would have been built in the town but it has not been found to date. It was possibly in the Old Station area where a number of Roman foundations were uncovered during the digging of air raid shelters in 1939. One of these was the second-largest bath-house found in Britannia (the largest is at Huggin Hill in London).

There is a plethora of religious inscriptions at Eboracum. An altar to Fortuna was set up by Sosia Iunicina, wife of an imperial legate and there are bronze plaques to Ocean and Tethys, brother and sister deities of the sea. One of the best preserved is a stone dedicated to Serapis, originally an Egyptian god, linked to the **VI Legion**.

By the time of *Britannia* it is likely that Eboracum was the command headquarters of the **Dux Britanniarum**. Most of the trouble in the late fourth century came from the north so it made sense to have the country's top general close at hand. By that time, too, Eboracum was either the capital of Britannia Secunda or Flavia Caesariensis. As with London, the lines of the Roman fortifications were retained in the Middle ages and in Eboracum, much of this is still standing. Various colonnaded buildings have been found under Trinity Lane and Micklegate and an altar there was dedicated to the genius Eboraci, the spirit of the town. These buildings may have been the basilica.

A possible bath house has been unearthed in Fetter Lane and there was a fountain in Bishophill Junior which implies a water supply, probably pumped from the Ouse. Terracotta pipes for this purpose have been found nearby.

By the time of *Britannia*, Eboracum, like Londinium, had its own bishop, Eborius, who attended the Arles council of 314. Some kind of public building linked with him, be it a basilica or church, has to lie undiscovered under the city's pavements.

No complete houses or shops have been excavated, but various objects imply a rich trading community which Eboracum already was before it became a colonia and the **VI** moved in. We know from inscriptions that the town had direct trading links with Burdigula (Bordeaux) and from jet jewellery found at Oppidum Ubiorum (Cologne), we can infer contact with the Rhineland. The Romans believed that Whitby jet had magical properties and there were extensive workshops in the Old Station area, with off-cuts and unfinished pieces having been found. In the fourth century, a parchment-yellow coloured pottery, now called Crambeck ware, was being produced. The town was also a thriving centre of the flax and linen trade, the damp soil ideal for growing the plant. Bodies in Eboracum burials dating from the *Britannia* period are wrapped in linen shrouds. Bronze and iron were widely worked too, one of the surviving gravestones (*stele*) of the period showing a smith in his workshop, complete with hammer and pincers.

The cemeteries at Eboracum are a fascinating source of information. In the *Britannia* period, many of the *stele* were re-used, as walls and insets for new buildings, which implies a certain irreverence, both for the past and the dead. This caused considerable disquiet and a law of **Theodosius the Great** moved to stop it happening. Even the tomb of Diocletian at Saloma (Split in today's Croatia) had been robbed. Over the whole time of Eboracum's Roman occupation, there were cremations and inhumations. In the latter case, where liquid gypsum was used, we are left with a ghostly imprint of the body and grave goods. A number of the inscriptions are to ex-soldiers of the **VI** or government officials and their families, the only people rich enough to have such monuments made. Poorer graves tended to be dug further away from the town centre, often strung out along the roads that led to it.

The bodies themselves give us age statistics. 15 per cent of the 350 excavated burials were of children; only a few were older than 45. The average height of a woman was 5ft 1in, of a man, 5ft 7in. DNA analysis has shown that the men in particular were as mixed a bunch as their Londinium counterparts, with Mediterranean origins. One body discovered in 2009 showed clearly that the deceased was a gladiator.

By the *Britannia* period, a general rise in sea level was having an effect on Eboracum. The nearby naval base at Brough-on-Humber (Petuaria) was abandoned soon after the middle of the fourth century and there is evidence of serious flooding at York (still a problem in 2015!) which would have destroyed the quays along the Ouse. The removal of the **VI** may have led to *foederati* being brought on to garrison the town and the fort itself may have been partially occupied by civilians.

... AND COUNTRY

... AND COUNTRY

'Then the Roman came with a heavy hand,
And bridged and roaded and ruled the land.'

The River's Tale
Rudyard Kipling

Sixty years ago, there was a school of thought that a squirrel could travel from Scotland to the south coast of England in Roman times without touching the ground once. We now know that this is plain wrong. There were certainly forests at the time of *Britannia*, larger and less travelled than today, but they were interspersed by treeless areas and open ground where farming, the traditional country economy, had been going on for centuries. Britannia was a wetter place than today. Allowing for today's on-going panic about climate-change worldwide, the disappearance of the polar ice and rising sea levels, this is not new. Fenlands were by no means confined to modern East Anglia, with the levels of Kent and Somerset particularly prone to flooding, as they still are. Braughing in Hertfordshire, perhaps an Iron Age centre of some importance, went through two serious flooding episodes along its valley floor and, as we have seen, Eboracum was also badly hit.

In terms of actual climate, the Britannia of the fourth century was warmer than today, perhaps similar to today's south of France. Procopius, in the fifth century, wrote, '... to the south of the Wall there is a salubrious air, changing with the seasons, being moderately warm in summer and cool in winter'. This is the same man, remember, who believed that it was impossible to survive for more than half an hour north of the Wall, so perhaps we should take his view with a pinch of salt! Vineyards have been found as far north as Yorkshire, without any of the artificial science which their modern equivalents use. That said, we know from archaeological and artistic evidence that the army in Britannia was equipped with 'winter gear' such as trousers and cloaks which implies that the country was still colder than much of the empire.

What difference did Roman occupation make to the wet forested land beyond the German Sea? Rudyard Kipling, writing with a poet's imagination early in the twentieth century, saw the 'ancient Britons' as a wild, hopeless lot who nevertheless had a certain charm. When the Romans arrived, imperial correctness was forced on them. Rectangular army camps sprang up everywhere; straight roads linked them. Towns had angular grid patterns. Old ways changed. The historical record confirms this – the emperor Hadrian, fascinated by *agri deserti*, abandoned countryside, carried out extensive land reclamation in the Fenlands; and he had the engineers to do it, which the Britons almost certainly did not.

Kipling's poem *The Land* however is probably closer to the truth. In it, whoever *owns* a particular piece of farming land, it is the locals who know its secrets and how to work it. He imagines a character called Hobdenius in the Roman period who evolves to Hobden under the Vikings and whose descendants are still farmers under George V in Kipling's own time. Gradual evolution is probably a better description for what happened in the five centuries of Roman occupation rather than the sudden culture shock of imperial rule. Engineers can only achieve so much – eight hundred years after the legions left, King John famously lost his crown jewels in the Wash, an area that Hadrian may already have thought he had reclaimed from the sea; five centuries later still, Oliver Cromwell was still trying to cope with rising sea levels there. In the countryside, it is usually nature, rather than the Roman, which rules!

There is no more disputed topic in Roman history than population size. In the 1920s, Roman Britain was believed to have less than a million inhabitants. In the 1930s, this crept up to a million and a half. Not until the 1950s was there a realistic shift in thinking.

The problem is that no central government statistics exist in Britain before the first census of 1801 (and even censi are, of course, inaccurate). Domesday Book of 1086-7 gives a partial picture, incomplete though the survey was, and it was never an actual head count. Given the Roman preoccupation with administration and its associated paperwork, tax collection surveys such as Tiberius' at the time of Christ's birth have yielded very little accurate information.

Using local studies of cemeteries and government records, such as they are, over the last sixty years, the smart money today is on the population of the fourth century being somewhere in the region of 5-6 million. This is very tentative and was subject to local de-population and the movement of people, although there is no evidence of migration from country to town which was a marked feature of the eighteenth century Industrial Revolution. With to-day's figure of sixty-five million in mind for the UK, one of the first things that would strike us if we could get hold of an H.G. Wells time-machine and pay a call to the fourth century, is how *empty* the place would seem.

The countryside's economy was all about food production. Much research has been carried out over the last fifty years into exactly how much would have to be grown, to sustain a population which was larger than we once believed and to feed an army in residence. The well-known comment by Ammianius (see HOW DO WE KNOW?) about British grain being shipped to the army in Germania under the emperor Julian implies that there was a surplus. But is that a one-off or was it the norm for the fourth century? Written sources can only take us so far. Archaeology, too, has its deficiencies. Studies of individual villas like Lullingstone in Kent, Fishbourne in Sussex and Brading in the Isle of Wight have produced a fascinating snapshot of the villa economy, but does this information apply to *all* villas or only those studied?

What research *has* proved is that there were extensive villages dotted around the country which had nothing to do with the villas. It has also shown that there was much more land under the plough than we once thought and the subsequent concentration of food production in the 'three-field' system of the Saxons was in many ways a backward step. The homes of villagers changed little, if at all, over the Roman period. The sunken, thatched-roof circular houses described in *Britannia* were identical to the ones that Julius Caesar saw in 54BC. The re-creations of them at Butser Hill in Hampshire give us an idea of their warmth and comfort. They did not have the mosaics and hypocausts of sophisticated Roman villas and town-houses but they were functional and the fact that they changed so little is proof of this.

The Romans brought no new technology with them in terms of farming. The heavy, iron-bladed plough was probably introduced from Gaul before the conquerors arrived. It would be yoked to oxen or men and the spring ploughing was a routine, if vital, part of the farmers' year. Wheat was grown, as were oats and barley, along with peas, beans and fodder for the animals – hay, vetch and turnips. Fruit was certainly cultivated – seeds of grapes and a wide variety of berries have been found in cesspits and rubbish dumps throughout the country.

In terms of animal husbandry, cattle and sheep were reared extensively. The raiding parties who regularly fought each other in pre-Roman times as well as those who hit the Wall in *Britannia* took such animals as their right – 'The mountain sheep are sweeter, but the valley sheep are fatter; We therefore deemed it meeter, to carry off the latter,' as *The War Song of Dinas Vawr*, written in 1829 by Thomas Love Peacock, has it. Horses were reared for war and for the hunt. Cattle provided beef, milk and hides. Sheep gave wool and mutton (until the nineteenth century, the cheapest meat). Wives and children tended the chickens and geese and collected the eggs. The pigs could be fed on the undergrowth of woodland, not needing grass like the other animals. What is different about the farming year in comparison with later centuries, is that there seems to have been no annual slaughter of animals. This routinely happened in the Middle Ages and well beyond because of a shortage of fodder over the winter. Romano-British settlements did not have this problem, so that meat was available all year round.

That said, life in the countryside was nasty, brutish and short. Villages and villas had to be self-sufficient. There was no charitable set-up by the infant Christian church and no government surplus in the way of food. The harvest was vital and the whole community took part in its collection. There is still considerable debate on the relationship between town and country. Was it essentially parasitic, with the towns demanding food supplies from the local villages? Or was the countryside stimulated by urban demand? Galloping inflation in the third century meant that by the time of *Britannia*, the government was commandeering goods and produce rather than the money obtained from selling in the market-place, the previous system.

For Roman farmers, various almanacs existed with tables for seasonal work. They are linked to the weather and the gods. To take one example, the first century expert Lucius Columella *On Agriculture* for May –

> '31 days. The Nones fell on the seventh day. The day has 14½ hours. The night has 9½ hours. The sun is in the sign of Taurus. The month is under the protection of Apollo. The grain fields are cleared of weeds. The sheep are shorn. The wool is washed. Young steers are put under the yoke. The vetch for fodder is cut. The lustration [ritual purification] of the grain field is made. Sacrifices to Mercury and Flora.'

If the rural round changed little over the period of Roman occupation of Britannia, a definite novelty was the villa, which came into its own in the *Britannia* era. Some of these country houses probably belonged to the decurions, the local government officials who would have owned a town house too. Apart from the villa proper which was a family home with quarters for servants/slaves, villa economy included an estate which would contain arable fields, pasture for animals, woodlands, a water supply and quite possibly one or more villages. Villas come in all shapes and sizes, but they are larger and more complex by the fourth century, implying that perhaps extended families or even several families occupied them, not unlike a small gated estate of today.

The 'public rooms' of these villas were over the top by modern standards. Walls were painted red, brown and green. Real and faux marble columns held up the roofs and colonnades. Gigantic mosaics covered the floors with scenes from Classical (often Greek) literature and religion. Some of them, like the cockerel-headed figure at Brading, are still obscure. The head with the Chi-Rho symbol from Hinton St Mary is clearly Christ, whereas the god often identified as Neptune at Verulamium is probably Cernunnos, the horned god of the Celts. If the décor was bright and fussy, furniture was sparse. The Romans ate lounging on couches (whatever that did to their digestion!) like the chaises longue of the eighteenth century. Wooden chests were used to hold linen. Tables and chairs were often folding to save space. Lighting was achieved by braziers of open fires or oil-filled terracotta lamps. The kitchen might have an oven, as at Silchester, or a grid-iron fixed over a charcoal fire on a platform. Pots and pans were made of copper and a variety of utensils have been found, including pastry cutters and pestles and mortars for grinding herbs and spices. The toilet was an earth closet outdoors, although it might have a roof and even walls for comfort and privacy. The most elaborate of the villas, for example that probably built for Tiberius Claudius Cogidubnus in the second century at Fishbourne, had complex bath houses and hypocausts.

What villas rarely had was any meaningful defence system, which left them vulnerable in the lawless years following the leaving of the legions. Such an attack forms part of the plot line of *Britannia III: The Warlords*.

DRAMATIS PER- SONAE VERI

DRAMATIS PER-SONAE VERI

the real people of *Britannia*

'Britain is a province fertile with tyrants.'

St Jerome, *Letters*

The three books of the *Britannia* series contain dozens of fictional characters (see COFFEE WITH DIOCLETIAN) and they also have a smattering of historical ones. Read all about them below. As with LOCATION, LOCATION, LOCATION the Roman numeral(s) refer to the book(s) of the series in which they appear.

Alaric the Goth, III

Alaric was a leader of the Visigoths, one of several nomadic tribes whose exact origin is unclear. It is probable that they came from what is today Russia, north of the Black sea and were themselves driven west by the spread of the Huns from still further east. Alaric was probably born along the Danube in today's Romania and served as a leader of *feoderati* (irregular, foreign troops) under **Theodosius the Great** in 394. His loyalty was not sufficiently recognized by the emperor and an embittered Alaric became an enemy, destroying towns all over modern Greece. He invaded Italy in 401 and was twice defeated by **Stilicho**. Even so, the senate was forced to pay huge subsidies to keep the Goths quiet. Alaric invaded Italy again on **Stilicho's** death in 408 and laid siege to Rome two years later. The gates were opened on 24 August and the usual three days of looting and pillage followed. Even so, deaths were relatively few and the Romans were treated humanely.

Alaric died months later attempting to invade Africa and he was buried with Visigothic ritual in the river Bucentius (Busento) in Calabria, Italy.

Andragathius, II

Andragathius was **Magnus Maximus'** *Magister Equitum* (cavalry commander) who captured and killed the emperor **Gratian** in 383. When **Maximus** was himself defeated five years later, Andragathius drowned himself. He may have been born in Spain and may have been a relative (some accounts say brother) of **Maximus** which may explain his suicide.

Calpurnius Succatus, II, III

The sparse facts about St Patrick give his father's name as Calpurnius and he was a decurion (government official) in Britannia. Nothing more is known about him.

Chrysanthos, I, II

Despite his prominence in the *Britannia* series, very little is known about the *vicarius Britanniarum*. He was the son of a bishop of Constantinople and had been governor of an Italian province before his British appointment.

Civilis (fl. 368) I

Civilis (his other names are not known) was vicarius of Britannia at the time of the Great Conspiracy in 367. Exactly who he was and what role he played in putting down the rebellion, is unknown.

Conchessa Succatus (fl. 400) II, III

St Patrick's mother was Conchessa, the wife of the decurion **Calpurnius**. Various accounts, none of them reliable, list her as a relative of Martin, the bishop of Caesarodunum (Tours) who himself became a saint with a shrine on the pilgrim's road to Santiago de Compostella in northern Spain.

Constantine III (d. 411) III

Flavius Claudius Constantinus was the third usurper in the space of two years to challenge the emperor **Honorius** for the throne. Like Constantine the Great, **Magnus Maximus**, **Marcus** and **Gratian** before him, Constantine was elected by the army after some kind of military coup. Like **Maximus**, he took British troops with him when he crossed to Bononia (Boulogne) in 407. Despite an initial defeat, he drove **Honorius**' troops back to Italy and set up his capital at Arelate (Arles). The death of **Stilicho** in the summer of 408 meant that Constantine could wage a successful war in Spain before turning on **Honorius** at **Ravenna**. **Honorius** panicked and appointed him co-emperor in the West.

Attacked by barbarians from the north, Constantine invaded Italy but was forced to pull back to Gaul by 410. In Britannia, there was a revolt against him in his absence and his officials were thrown out. By the summer of 411, his luck had run out. He was captured and executed on his way to **Ravenna**.

Elen Luyddog (fl. late fourth century) II, III

Elen of the Armies has never officially been canonized but she is regarded as a saint (Helen of Caernarfon) in the Welsh church. Her father was **Eudaf,** a British chieftain based near **Segontium** (Caernarfon) and according to the twelfth century folk tales the *Mabinogion*, married **Magnus Maximus**, whom her people (probably the **Deceangli** tribe) called Macsen Wledig. Her sobriquet Llwyddog possibly refers to the building of military roads across what is now Wales, although she may have led men personally in battle. Some accounts say she died in Caernarfon in 388 but as this is the date of **Maximus'** death, it seems too pat, unless suicide is supposed.

Eudaf (fl. late fourth century) II

Eudaf Hen (the Old) was the father of **Elen Llwyddog** and perhaps used the Latinized name Octavius. Geoffrey of Monmouth's account in the thirteenth century confuses the man with another local chieftain at the time of Constantine the Great, a hundred years before the *Britannia* era.

Flavius Gratianus Augustus (359-383) II

Gratian was the eldest son of **Valentinian I** and accompanied his father on various campaigns on the Rhine and Danube. Born in Sirimania (today's Sremska Mitrovica in Serbia) he became emperor in 367. On **Valentinian's** death in 375, Gratian effectively ruled both halves of the empire, although nominally the emperor in the east was his half-brother **Valentinian II.** Under pressure from all sides, he effectively gave the eastern empire to **Theodosius the Great** in 379.

He alienated his troops by appearing in foreign armour on parades and upset traditionalist Romans by vicious attacks on paganism. Under Gratian's orders, temples were destroyed all over the empire and even the 'untouchable' Vestal Virgins were sent packing. He was defeated in the power struggle with **Magnus Maximus**, and possibly murdered by **Andragathius** in August 383.

Fullofaudes (fl. 367) I

The soldier-historian Ammianus Mercellinus (see HOW DO WE KNOW?) mentions Fullofaudes in his *Res Gestae* covering the years 353-378. He was **Dux Britanniarum** in 367, the year of the Great Conspiracy which forms the action of *Britannia I: The Wall.* It is not clear from Ammianius whether Fullofaudes was besieged or killed in the rebellion, but his name has vanished by 369. He may have been from the Rhineland as were an increasing number of troops fighting for Rome in this period.

Gratian, III

Geoffrey of Monmouth, writing in the twelfth century, refers in his *Historia Regum Britanniae* (History of the Kingdom of Britain) to Gracianus Municeps, who ruled Britannia after the death of **Magnus Maximus**. Since Geoffrey's *Historia* is largely fiction, it is not helpful in getting to the truth. He followed **Marcus** as a usurper, aiming to topple the emperor **Honorius**.

Magnus Maximus (Macsen Wledig) (c. 335-388) I, II

Maximus was born in Gallaecia, Spain and some accounts claim that he was the nephew of **Count Theodosius** whom he may have accompanied to Britannia in 368. He served with distinction under the Count in Africa in 373 and along the Danube three years later. He was back in Britannia in 380 and put down an invasion of the Picts and Scots.

In 383, Maximus was proclaimed emperor by his British troops and sailed for Gaul to stake his claim against **Gratian**. He took British troops with him, beginning the stripping of the country's defences which would eventually be disastrous. Maximus defeated **Gratian** in battle near Paris and the emperor was killed at Lugdunum (Lyon) in August of the same year. His advance into Italy was stopped by the **younger Theodosius**, now Eastern Emperor and in the negotiations that followed, Maximus was acknowledged as Emperor in the West. His capital was **Augusta Treverorum** (Trier) and he was a popular ruler.

By 388, Maximus was fighting again against Valentinian II and he was defeated by **Theodosius** at Save, the first time that the Huns fought for the Romans. He was finally defeated and executed at Aquileia in northern Italy and the Roman senate passed a decree of *Damnatio Memoriae* against him, which means that he was effectively airbrushed from history. His brother Marcellinus was killed in the campaign and his son Flavius was strangled on **Theodosius'** orders. His female family members were spared although there is some doubt as to who his wife was.

Maximus becomes a legendary figure in various early Welsh accounts. The *Dream of Macsen Wledig* from the *Mabinogion* (twelfth century accounts of Welsh history) tells of his marriage to **Elen Luyddog** and the birth of a daughter.

Gold Solidus of Magnus Maximus minted at Augusta Treverorum (Trier) about 385. The inscription reads 'DN [Dominus – lord] Mag Maximus PF [Pius Filius – Faithful Son] Aug [Augustus – emperor]'.

Marcus (d. 407) III

Only the single name survives of the first of three usurpers in 406-7. The fact that there were so many, points up the chaotic, lawless nature of the time. External attacks on the empire and a lack of central authority, meant that anybody felt they could try their luck. Marcus was a soldier proclaimed by the army (see **Magnus Maximus**) in 406, but he soon fell foul of the troops who had elevated him and they killed him.

Nectarides (d 367) I

The man is referred to by Ammianus in *Res Gestae* as being **Comes Litori Saxonii (Count of the Saxon Shore)** and that he was killed during the Great Conspiracy of 367.

Niall of the Nine Hostages (fl. 400) III

Early Irish history is cluttered with legend and there is no full agreement that Niall was actually a real person! Various annals place his death in the 380s, 390s or 411 – in *Britannia*, we have gone for the last one. According to legend, he was the fifth and youngest son of Eochaid Mugmedon, the high king of Ireland. His mother, Cairenn, was perhaps Romano-British.

The nine hostages of his name *may* refer to tribute given by the five provinces of Ireland (Ulaid, Mumu, Connacht, Mide and Laigin) and one each from the Scots, Saxons and Franks. One account says that he frequently raided the west and south coasts of Britannia and that he captured the boy who would become St Patrick. One account of his life says that he was drowned on his way home from a raid, perhaps attacked at sea by a Roman patrol.

Patrick (fl. Fifth century) II, III

There are particular problems researching people who become saints! Accredited with miracles long after their deaths, they acquire a status in which any implausible fact is attributed to them. This is especially true of national patron saints. Think of St Patrick and we immediately have notions of shamrocks and driving the snakes out of Ireland!

His father was **Calpurnius**, a decurion stationed in Britannia and he may have been kidnapped by pirates (perhaps even **Niall of the Nine Hostages**) when he was sixteen. After six years as a slave, Patrick escaped and got back to Britain before returning, after visions of God, as a Christian missionary to pagan Ireland. There are large numbers of Patrick-related sites in Ireland and inevitably his life has become hopelessly intertwined with legend.

Pelagius (c. 354-418) I, II, III

Pelagius was born in Britannia (some accounts say Ireland) and was a fluent writer of Latin and Greek. Moving to Rome about 380, he became known for his austerity and was critical about the lack of morality he saw about him. Opposing the idea of predestination and pushing the notion of free will, he fell foul of the orthodox Christianity of his day (see SO MANY GODS) and was declared a heretic. He survived **Alaric's** sack of Rome in 410 and moved to Cartago (Carthage) and them to Hierosolyma (Jerusalem). He was excommunicated in 418 and was kicked out of the city, probably dying in Egypt in the same year. The man was despised for centuries. One seventeenth century Calvinist (for whom, of course, predestination was everything) calls him 'Accurst Pelagius'. Only in our own time do his views seem reasonable.

Stilicho (c. 359-408) III

Flavius Stilicho was the son of a Vandal soldier and a Roman woman. He joined the army and rose through the ranks under **Theodosius the Great**. In 383, he was the emperor's envoy to the court of the Persian king Shapur III and was promoted to *Magister Militum* (general) soon afterwards. He married **Theodosius'** niece Serena, the marriage producing three children.

Clearly a soldier of considerable ability, Stilicho won a great victory at Frigidus in September 394 where his comrade was **Alaric** the Goth who would later become his enemy. When **Theodosius** died the following year, Stilicho became the guardian of the boy-emperor **Honorius**. The rest of his career was a series of brilliant campaigns and political outmanoeuvrings, dogged by the jealousy of the court. About 398, Stilicho may have been in Britannia, stopping an invasion by the Picts.

Three years later, he defeated **Alaric** at **Pollentia** on Easter Sunday and captured the Goth's wife and children. He beat him again at Verona the following year. In 406 a confederacy of tribes, the Vandals, the Alans and the Suebi crossed the Rhine putting huge pressure on the western empire. The usurper **Constantine III** invaded at the same time and Stilicho had to seal off the passes through the Alps to keep him out of Italy. Forced to conclude a peace with **Alaric**, Stilicho lost support and was ousted by a coup in the summer of 408. He was executed, along with his son, on 22 August.

Count Theodosius (c. 310-376) I

Flavius Julius Theodosius claimed descent from Julius Caesar's family at a time when such ties were important. In the late Republic and early Empire, the *equites* formed the wealthy nobility and were the political and military leaders of the state. He was born in Gallaecia, Spain and married Flavia Thermantia, probably in the 330s and had at least two sons, Honorius and **Theodosius**, both born at Cauca (Segovia) in Spain. The family was Christian.

Sent to Britannia in 368 with the rank of *Comes* (Count) his job was to put down the native rebellion of the previous year. This he did with efficiency and returned to the court of the emperor Valentinian I with promotion to *Magister Equitum* (cavalry commander). He campaigned against the Alemanni from Swabia in today's Germany in 370 and took on another revolt in Mauretania (today's Morocco) three years later. Soon afterwards, Theodosius seems to have fallen foul of the new emperor, **Gratian** – the details are unclear – and he was arrested and taken to Cartago (Carthage in modern Tunisia) where he was executed in 376.

Theodosius I (the Great) (347-95) I, II, III

Flavius Theodosius was the son of **Count Theodosius** born at Cauca, Gallaecia, Spain, probably in January 347. He fought his first campaign alongside his father in the Great Conspiracy in Britannia in 367. Seven years later we find him directing military operations against the Sarmatians and Alemanni in Moesia (today's Serbia) on the Danube. When his father was disgraced and executed, Theodosius 'retired' (probably for his own safety) to the family home in Spain. In the complicated politics of the Tetrarchy, the death of the emperor Valentinian I in 375 saw his sons Valentinian II and **Gratian** co-ruling in the west. Valens, Emperor in the East was killed at Adrianople in 378 and **Gratian** appointed Theodosius Emperor in the East. After **Maximus** defeated **Gratian**,

Theodosius appointed his own son **Arcadius** to co-rule in the east. After 392, Theodosius ruled as sole Emperor, a brief period of status quo before the empire started to disintegrate.

An ardent Christian and patron of the arts, Theodosius' failure to remove the Gothic threat led to **Alaric's** ultimate attack on Rome in 410.

Valentinus (fl. 367-9) I

According to Ammianus Marcellinus, Valentinus was a Pannonian (from today's Hungary) who was a court favourite of the emperor Valentinian I. He was exiled to Britannia for some unknown crime and led the Great Conspiracy in 367, presumably for reasons of revenge. Ammianus' account says that he was executed by the **Dux Brittanniarum**, Dulcitius.

The Vandal general Stilicho, from an ivory bas relief in the cathedral in Monza. The haircut is still that of Julius Caesar, despite the fact that this carving was made about 400. Note the obvious 'crossbow' cloak clasp and the tight leggings which are Germanic. The heads portrayed on his shield are the boy emperors he had sworn to protect.

UNDER A DIFFERENT SKY

UNDER A DIFFERENT SKY

The Tribes of Britannia

… 'all the rest of mankind that we have been believed to dwell on a different earth and under a different sky …'
Cassius Dio's version of Boudicca's speech to her troops
Manduessedum 61 AD

We first hear about them from Julius Caesar. They were the tribes of Britannia and they beat him back at the coast, somewhere near Pevensey, in 55BC. They were probably the Regni, whose territory extended from Southampton Water west to the borders of East Sussex or Kent.

The fact that the native Celts had no written language means that there is a huge hole in the historical record and in our understanding of them. The names of the tribes are Latin, given to them by the Romans. We can guess where most of their capitals were by the Roman place names – Winchester was Venta Belgarum, the market place of the Belgae; Norwich was Venta Icenorum, the market place of the Iceni and so on. The tribes saw each other as rivals and their borders, probably marked by prominent geographical features like rivers, forests or rocky outcrops, must have changed constantly as they fought each other for territory, slaves, women and livestock. One of the major reasons for the successful invasion of Britannia was that the Romans were able to divide and conquer, picking these tribes off one by one. So while Boudicca of the Iceni went to war with Rome in her rebellion of 60AD, her sister queen Cartimandua of the **Brigantes** stayed loyal to the conquerors. What makes the rebellion of 367 (the theme of *The Wall*) so terrifying is that, for the first time, the tribes banded together. On a larger scale, the alliance of Goths, Vandals, Alans, Suebi, Saxons and Franks brought the western Roman Empire down in the fifth century.

Our counties (Norman creations based on earlier Saxon shires) are so long-established now that it is difficult to see beyond them, to names that have vanished and archaeological sites yet to be discovered.

All the tribes listed by Caesar and those referred to by later writers were almost certainly still there by the time of *Britannia* but it is anybody's guess how far they had intermarried with each other and with the Romans themselves by that period. The phrase Romano-British is infuriatingly vague but it is all we have. It includes client kings like Cogidubnus who got so comfortably into bed with the conquerors that they gave him several *civitae* (cities) to rule. It includes merchants who imported wine, grain, salt, earthenware, jewellery and a whole host of luxuries from elsewhere in the empire. Gradually, over four hundred years, all the tribes of modern England and Wales and some in Lowland Scotland learned to live alongside the Romans, benefiting in many ways from being part of the greatest empire in the ancient world.

The Celts were not the original inhabitants of Britannia, having migrated from the east rather as the various 'barbarian' peoples were to do from the fourth century onwards. They were a vibrant people, fierce and proud, warriors and poets, thinkers and lovers, like any people are. How quickly and how deeply they identified with the Roman empire is anybody's guess. Each tribe had its own ruling elite (unlike the Romans, open to women), its priests and faith, its warrior class, its artisans and craftsmen, its farmers and hunters.

In this book we can only scratch the surface of those people who lived 'under a different sky' – words put into Boudicca's mouth by the Roman historian Cassius Dio – and we have concentrated only on the tribes specifically mentioned in *Britannia*. Their languages and their religion are discussed elsewhere (see WHO SPOKE WHAT and SO MANY GODS).

NB – there is so much disagreement about the meaning of tribal names that we have omitted this altogether.

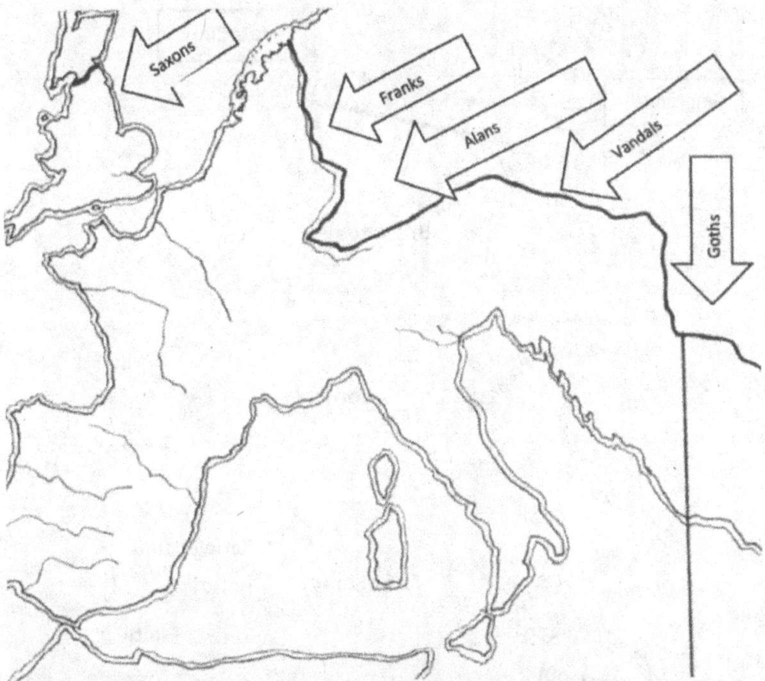

Map 4: *The empire under attack. Increasingly, from the middle of the fourth century, various 'barbarian' tribes invaded the empire from the north, ultimately sweeping away five hundred years of Roman civilization.*

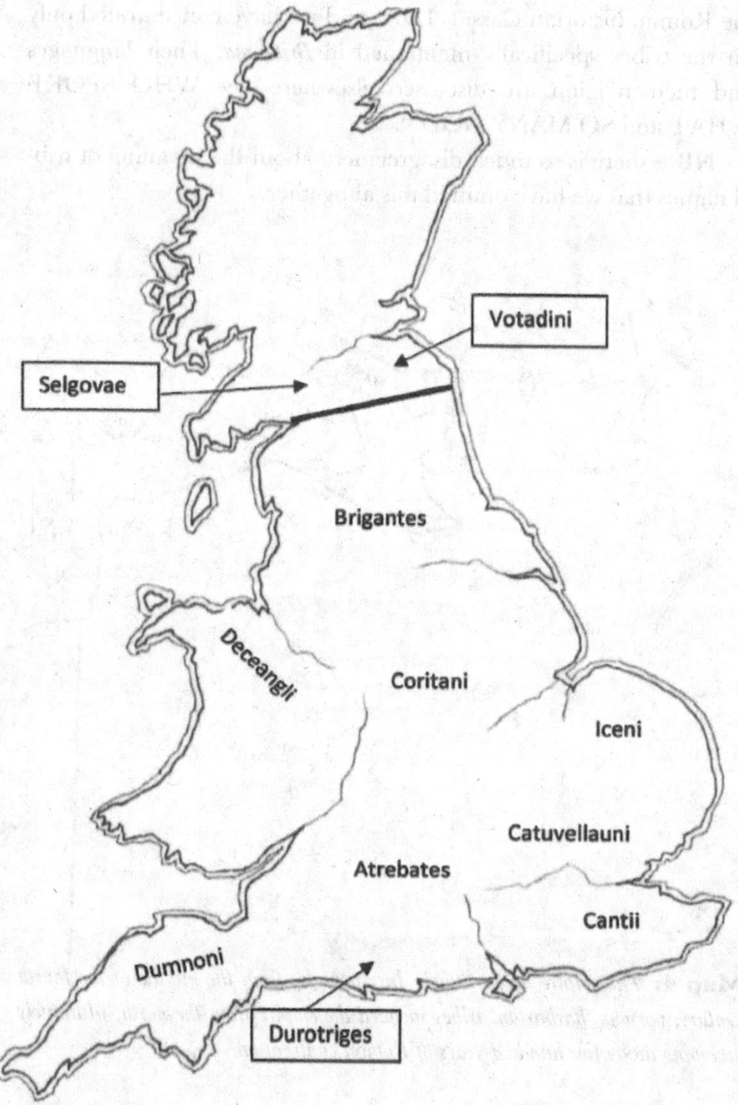

Map 5: *The main tribes mentioned in the* Britannia *series. This map shows the areas occupied by the tribes, although of course, territories were not finite and boundaries constantly shifted.*

Atrebates

Caesar mentions this tribe and had probably already met them in his war in Gaul (*de Bello Gallico*). The British 'branch' may have been led by a king called Commius and they settled in today's Hampshire, Berkshire and West Sussex. Their tribal capital was **Calleva Atrebatum**, Silchester. Their later ruler was the grandly named crawler Tiberius Clodius Cogidubnus and the tribe appears to have been a well-behaved client kingdom from the first century onwards.

Brigantes

A huge tribe, perhaps a confederation, south of **Hadrian's Wall** centring on Yorkshire. Including the list of the geographer Ptolemy, (the writer carried out a survey of the Empire in his *Geographia* c. 150AD), there are no less than fourteen known settlements, many of which have now been excavated. Their most famous queen was Cartimandua, a shrewd politician of the first century who played the Romans and other tribal leaders off against each other.

Catuvellauni

Like the **Atrebates**, the Catuvellauni may have come from Gaul shortly before Julius Caesar's arrival on Britannia's south coast. Ptolemy records their capital at Verlamion, later **Verulamium**, today's St Albans. The tribe produced two famous leaders, both of whom made life hell for the Romans. One was Cunobelinus, who became Shakespeare's *Cymbeline* and the other Caratacus, taken to Rome as a prisoner of war. He so impressed the Senate with his nobility that he and his family were allowed to live in the city in peace.

Cornovii

The Cornovii's territory, as listed by Ptolemy, covered today's Cheshire, Shropshire, Staffordshire, Herefordshire and the Welsh county of Powys. **Deva**, Chester, and **Viroconium Cornoviorum**, Wroxeter, were the major centres, military and civil.

Deceangli

The tribe occupied territory in north-east Wales, today's Clwyd. It is possible that the *civitas* stood at Caerhun (today a fourteenth century churchyard) called Canovium, although this may have been merely an army fort. Lead and silver were mined here, one example weighing 192lb having been discovered in Chester. Unlike the more warlike Ordovices and Silures tribes further south in Wales, the Deceangli seem to have been on friendly terms with the Romans throughout the period.

Dumnonii

The tribe lived in the far west, in today's Cornwall and Devon. Ptolemy discusses them, as does the Antonine Itinerary. The Capital was **Isca Dumnoniiorum**, today's Exeter, which began as the headquarters of the **II Augusta** legion. No villas have been found here and there are only scattered farmsteads, but the area's economy may have been based on tin mining and the trading of that metal with Armorica (today's Britanny).

Durotriges

Another confederation, living in today's Dorset, Wiltshire, Somerset and Devon. At the time of *Britannia*, the capital was **Durnovaria**, today's Dorchester. We know from the historian Suetonius that they fought against Vespasian's **II Augusta** legion in 43AD and their hill fort at Maiden Castle remains one of the most impressive in the country. Recent archaeological research, Bournemouth University's Durotriges Project, has uncovered round houses, storage pits and two substantial Roman villas.

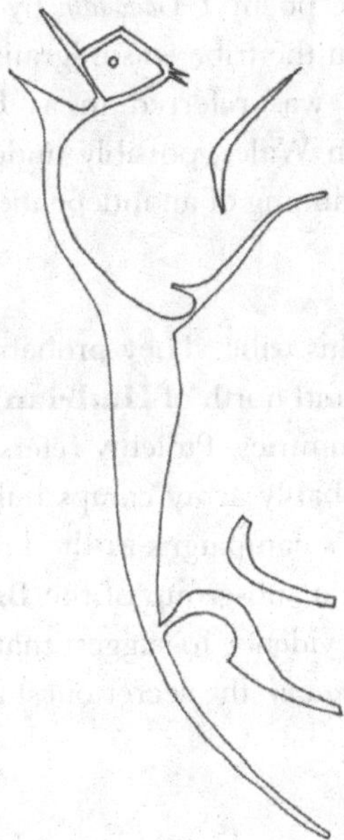

The Uffington White Horse, Oxfordshire. Carved into the hillside to reveal the chalk, this was probably a tribal totem and was adopted nearly two thousand years later by the Berkshire Yeomanry. County boundaries have since changed so that Uffington is now in Oxfordshire.

Gabrantovices

A shadowy group referred to by Ptolemy that perhaps lived in to-day's Yorkshire. They may have been a sub-group of the **Brigantes**.

Gododdin (Votadini)

The tribe lived north of **Hadrian's Wall** in the *Britannia* period and their capital was **Din Paladyr**, today's Traprain Law. The Romans called them the Votadini and they were effectively a buffer state between the northern province of **Britannia Secunda** and the Picts of the Highlands. Various archaeological finds at Traprain and elsewhere indicate a degree of trade with the empire.

The sixth century epic poem *Y Gododdin* by the bard Aneurin was written at a time when the tribe was migrating south to Wales. Their original homeland was referred to as Hen Ogledd (Old North) and their arrival in Wales, possibly under Cunedda, is regarded by some as the beginning of an independent Welsh culture.

Selgovae

Only Ptolemy mentions this tribe. They probably lived in what is today south-western Scotland north of **Hadrian's Wall** – present-day Kirkcudbright and Dumfries. Ptolemy refers to four *civitates* by name, but these were probably army camps built to maintain the *Pax Romana* after Agricola's campaigns in the first century. It may be that the Selgovae were a sub-group of the **Brigantes** south of the Wall. There is strong evidence to suggest that the Selgovae and the **Gododdin** provided *arcani* (the secret ones) as spies and scouts in the *Britannia* era.

Trinovantes

A tribe living in today's Essex and Suffolk, they may have been the most powerful of the tribes in Julius Caesar's time. Their capital was possibly originally at Braughing in Hertfordshire, today a small village, but archaeology has not confirmed this. By the time of *Britannia*, it was **Caesaromagus**, Chelmsford, with another important base at **Camulodunum**, Colchester.

Votadini – see Gododdin

SO MANY GODS

SO MANY GODS

'So many gods, so many creeds,
So many paths that wind and wind
While just the art of being kind
Is all the sad world needs.'

Ella Wheeler Wilcox 1855-1919

Native Gods

Religion in the period covered by *Britannia* is chaotic. The native Celts had a pantheon of gods and goddesses as all ancient peoples had, personified deities for things they did not understand and which frightened them. There were gods of thunder, lightning, fire and every weather system known to man. Gods blessed – or did not bless, according to their whims – the all-important harvest. They presided over the hunt and flew, vengeful, over battlefields. They controlled the sun, the moon, the stars, all life and death.

The Celts probably had a 'high god', the rough equivalent of the Roman Jupiter, and lesser deities who often turn up in groups of three. Cernunnos, the horned god, may be equated with fertility and he morphed into Satan in Christian philosophy. Animals were important – Epona was a Roman horse goddess; wild boars and even hares were worshipped. Certain places were holy, especially woodland groves and springs. Coventina was a water goddess from **Brocolitia** on **Hadrian's Wall**, an example of a deity that may have been intensely local.

The *Britannia* series focuses above all on the Gododdin tribe whose most important god was Belatucadros. The name translates as 'fair, shining one' and he was probably linked with the sun. There is also a suggestion that the Romans equated him with the war god, Mars. In the context of the barbarian invaders of the period (see THE ENEMIES) the Hibernian/Gaelic god referred to is Dagda. In Irish mythology he is the equivalent of Jupiter, leader of the Tuatha de Danaan, the pantheon of gods, has a bottomless cauldron of food and a war club that can both kill and restore life.

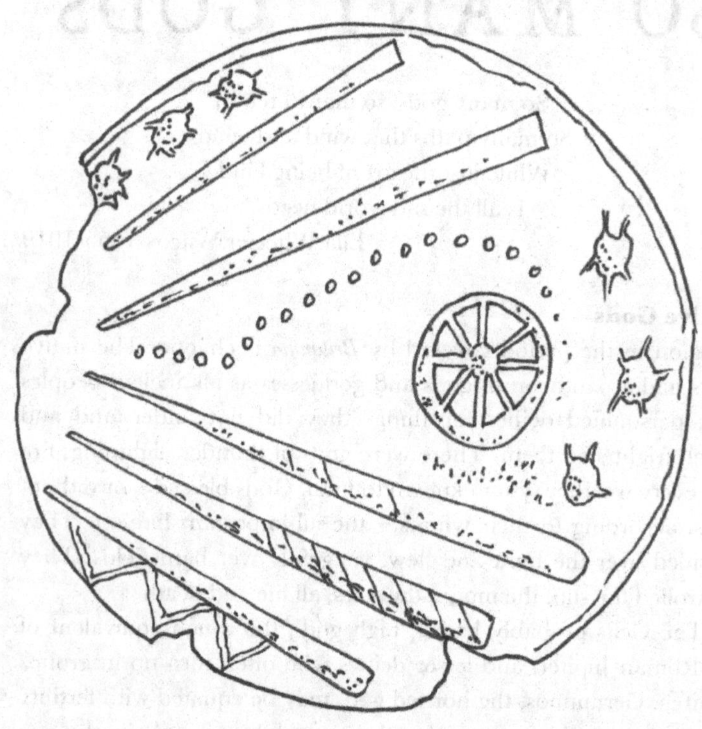

Votive coin or medallion connected with the Celtic god Taranis (thunder). The stars clearly show the heavens and the wheel possibly represents the rays of the sun. First century BC.

The Gods of Rome

Then the Romans came and it all began again! The crucial difference is that the Romans had a written language so the Graeco-Roman pantheon seems more ordered and sensible. The Celts made images of their gods and gave them names which were subsumed by Latin. The Romans made images too, but their superior artwork, in the statues of the forums, the columns of the temples and the wall-paintings of their houses, made it all the more acceptable. Jupiter, Mars, Diana, Vulcan, Ceres – they all looked like mortal men and women and so could pass almost unnoticed when they interfered in peoples' lives.

The problem, as the historian Guy de la Bedoyere points out, is that 'it is almost impossible to measure the quality and nature of symbolism, ritual and belief. One man's religious symbol is another man's decorative motif and yet another man's nightmare.' Suetonius Paulinus' legions destroyed the altars on Mona (Anglesey) and slaughtered the priests, the druids, who worshipped there. This was probably not as a result of an inherent detestation of foreign gods, but a realisation that the priesthood would foment anti-Roman feeling forever unless they were stopped.

In Rome and other major cities of the empire, Christians became the victims of pogroms organized by the state and, at least according to the nineteenth century novelists and Hollywood, were routinely thrown to the lions. This was not because Christianity was in itself a dangerous doctrine, but because worship of one God in place of many and following Christ undermined Roman traditions and the deified position of the emperor.

All over Roman Britannia we are still finding shrines, temples, amulets and graves which bear testimony to the faith of the period. The army camps are littered with shrines to Mithras; cities were associated with certain gods; Roman matrons prayed to no less than fifteen gods of the household to keep their families safe and well.

For the purposes of this book, we will discuss just those gods who are mentioned in the *Britannia* series. Did the people of the time actually believe in them? We live today in a cynical, materialistic world in which magic is mere illusion and in which everything can be explained by rationalism and science. It is difficult to imagine a time when this was not so. And our modern view might agree with the Roman poet Juvenal who wrote, 'You'd be no goddess, Fortuna, if there was any sense. *We* made you a spirit and set you in the sky.'

In the *Britannia* series, three deities get more mention than the others: Sol Invictus; Jupiter; and Mithras, imported from the east. The other faith which was a new arrival at the time, and also from the East, is Christianity and it is one of the mysteries of history why this obscure and demanding sect should have become *the* religion of the West.

The earliest representation of Christ in Britain. This mosaic from the floor of the villa at Hinton St Mary, Dorset, shows Jesus as a Roman, complete with toga, Caesar haircut and the Chi Rho sign behind him.

Christianity

Because Christianity is now the established faith of the western world, it is difficult to put it into the context of the *Britannia* series. At that point, in the late fourth century, it was already the official religion of the state but there were complications.

The story of Jesus is so well known that we have to remind ourselves that his existence rests largely on the Gospels, four books copied from each other and translated from Hebrew to Greek to Latin to English. There *are* other references to the man outside the Bible, but these are fragmented and contradictory. Attempts by modern historians and archaeologists to establish more about his life and death have not been impressive. And of course, individual faith kicks in almost at once. If you are a Christian, you will accept that Jesus was the son of God and that he rose from the dead. If you are not, you might be tempted to assume that he was just another of the incomprehensible misfits whom society branded mad.

According to the Bible, Jesus was born in Galilee, then part of the Roman province of Judea, in the reign of the emperor Tiberius. He was crucified, the usual punishment for slaves and rebels, on the orders of the prefect Pontius Pilate in the year his followers calculated as 33AD. These followers, the disciples, spread the word of his beliefs and teachings; and cults grew up in Rome and various parts of the Empire. There was certainly persecution by the state against Christians, largely because worship of a god who was not the emperor was a form of sedition that could not be tolerated. The Thracian cult of Dionysus, whom the Romans called Bacchus, was treated in the same way; its drunken, orgiastic adherents were slaughtered in a pogrom in 186BC.

What was different about Christianity was that it offered personal salvation. Trust in God was a ticket to heaven and increasingly, it was that afterlife, not our existence on earth, that mattered. Unlike **Mithraism** it was open to all. Jesus himself had been a rebel, taking on the Pharisees and clearing the temple. His disciples were poor men, fishermen and peasants. Over three centuries, this obscure cult, with its notions of peace and charity, rose to eminence when the emperor Constantine embraced it. At the battle of the Milvian Bridge in 312, the emperor's battle-cry to his troops was 'In this sign, conquer' and the sign was the Chi-Rho, the looped Greek cross of Christ. Constantine himself remained ambivalent – like any shrewd politician at any time, he hedged his bets, worshipping Christ and **Sol Invictus** side by side. It may be, in fact, that he conflated the two.

By the time of *Britannia*, despite the work of traditionalists like the emperor Julian to restore the old gods, Christianity was the religion of the state across the empire. **Theodosius the Great** in particular passed decrees to outlaw the worship of the *lares* and *penates*, the household gods which were probably of greater importance to the average 'Roman' than **Jupiter** and the rest. Romans believed that their homes had a spiritual presence – the *genius loci* – which protected families. An enforced alien faith, depending on a belief in miracles – water into wine, resurrection etc – did not sit well with that. Christianity was particularly rejected by the army, to whom **Mithras** was central. There are no archaeological examples of Christian shrines at any military base in Britannia.

In terms of structure, the early Christian church was linked with the politically powerful. There were probably chapels in the larger villas but the bishops are associated with the cities. Churches themselves were not purpose-built. In some cases, civic buildings were adapted; in others, private houses were used. Most Roman liturgy (except **Mithraism**) took place in the open air and it may have been the British weather that drove the Christians indoors.

Above all, we cannot assume that the Christians actually followed Christ's teaching, any more than they do today. Having been persecuted themselves, they became the persecutors, destroying Mithraic temples and doing their best to eradicate rival faiths.

The Pelagian Heresy

Pelagius appears in all three books of the *Britannia* series as the acceptable face of Christianity. The Christian church was obsessed with heresies – deviation from what they believed to be Christ's teaching – and this continued throughout the Middle Ages to the Reformation and to the myriad sects of today.

Pelagius' own beliefs were probably exaggerated by others, especially after his death and modern scholarship takes a more rational view of him. He was condemned at the Councils of **Cartago** (Carthage), in 411 and 418, especially by Augustine of Hippo because he stressed man's free will and did not accept the notion of predestination, believing that by good works man could free himself of Adam's original sin.

Jupiter

In the *Britannia* series, the phrase 'Jupiter highest and best' is used as an oath of exasperation, rather as many people say 'Jesus' today. Jupiter Optimus Maximus was only one name by which the king of the gods was known because he was the most omnipotent deity in the Roman pantheon. Tall and full-bearded, he is the Roman equivalent of the Greek Zeus and there were temples to him all over the empire. He was particularly associated with the sky and thunder – the lightning of storms were his thunderbolts. The designs have been found on legionary shields of the first century and invariably appear in epic Hollywood reconstructions. The eagle was Jupiter's favoured bird and the eagle became synonymous with empire. Every legion carried a silver eagle into battle and it adorned thousands of military and civic buildings across the empire. So powerful was this motif that it was copied in later centuries by any number of powers from Russia to the United States.

Jupiter Highest and Best. A bust of the king of the gods from Otricoli, near Rome.

Mithras 'also a soldier' from the Mithraeum in Londinium (London) destroyed by the Christians in the fourth century. (Museum of London)

Mithras

If **Sol Invictus** has military associations, the cult of Mithras is even more embedded in the army. Like Christianity, often seen as Mithraism's rival, it came from the east, specifically Persia (today's Iran and Iraq). We have no idea what liturgy and rituals were involved, either in initiation or regular services but there are dozens of shrines to the god in Britannia, usually in or near army camps. The cult was elitist and secret, so it appealed to army officers and perhaps to businessmen (the best known mithraeum in London was probably linked with them). Because of the secret element, its temples were dark and underground, made to resemble caves. Whatever ritualistic elements were involved, they included the slaughter of a bull – animal sacrifice was common in a variety of Roman and other cultures in the ancient world. Archaeological finds show Mithras in a Phrygian cap, kneeling on the back of a bull and cutting its throat. He wears a cape that hides the secrets of eternity and in some examples, spaces in the carving behind the god indicate that a lamp was once hung there to illuminate the scene. Two minor gods, Cautes and Cautopates, are often portrayed with him.

The archaeological evidence in Britannia indicates that mithraea were systematically destroyed, probably in the late fourth or early fifth century. It may be that this was the work of the Christians or the result of an imperial edict by one of the more muscular of the Christian emperors like **Theodosius the Great**. Experts cannot agree on when or why the cult came to an end but the dominance of Christianity and the removal of the legions have to be factors in this.

Sol Invictus

There is a lot of controversy today whether the cult of the Unconquered Sun is an offshoot of **Mithraism** or a standalone religion. It became official under the rule of emperor Aurelian in 274, various emperors wearing a crown of the sun's rays as late as Constantine. The last known inscription to the god dates from 387 but Augustine, the Christian missionary, was still preaching against him in the fifth century.

There is debate, too, about the cult's day. The *dies matalis solis invicti* (the sun god cult's birthday) was 25 December, part of Saturnalia, the Roman midwinter solstice. It is highly likely that the early Christian church claimed this as Christ's day to take advantage of a pre-existing holy day. This view is challenged today but the alternative possibility, that it actually was Christ's birthday is based on a dubious calculation from the date of the annunciation on the vernal equinox.

Further muddying of the waters arises from the parallels between Sol and Jesus. The halo attributed to Christ (and later, his saints) can be equated with the sun's rays; the twelve disciples with the cyclical signs of the zodiac and so on. All we can say with certainty is that, like **Mithras**, Sol Invictus was a popular cult with the army in the *Britannia* period.

Isis

There was a temple to this Egyptian goddess in Londinum which features in *Britannia III: the Warlords*. Because Egypt became part of the empire under Augustus, several of its gods and goddesses migrated, suitably Latinized, to other parts. She was associated with wisdom and understanding and statues of her with her son Horus easily blended into the Christian iconography of Madonna and Child.

FOLLOWING THE EAGLE

FOLLOWING THE EAGLE

'Legate, I come to you in tears – my cohort ordered home.
I've served in Britain forty years – what should I do in Rome?'
The Roman Centurion's Song
Rudyard Kipling

Most 'fact' books on the Roman army – and there are many of them – concentrate on the earlier centuries when the legions were the most formidable fighting force in the world. By the time of the *Britannia* series, the army was not what it was and its own structure meant that it could no longer hold the empire together. This, coupled with the fact that detailed organizational information is sparse for the period, gives us problems in analysing this vitally important aspect of Roman Britain.

Let us start with the army of the Principate, the army of Julius Caesar that morphed into that of the first Roman Emperor, Octavian Augustus. This is the Roman army of Hollywood, with its overlapping plate armour (*lorica segmentata*), its convex rectangular shields (*scuti*), its short stabbing swords (*gladii*), daggers (*pugia*), two throwing spears (*pila*) and hob-nailed sandals (*caligae*). This armour and equipment was highly suitable for Mediterranean warfare and formed the basic physical appearance of the legions. Incidentally, the over-use of scarlet, for tunics, shields and plumes is almost pure Hollywood. In the rare instances of military cloth having been found by archaeologists, the colour is usually off-white.

The strength of the Principate's army lay in the legions, a unit that today would be considered a regiment, traditionally 6,000 strong. Until 262, legionaries (*pedes*) were Roman citizens and most of them were volunteers. If they survived the rigours of twenty years campaigning they would be given a plot of land in lieu of a pension. The more celebrated of them owned a couple of slaves and had expensive graves stones (*stele*) made for them, like that of Marcus Favonius Facilis in Camulodunum, (Colchester).

Attached to the legions were the auxiliary units, non-Roman in origin and increasingly providing the cavalry (*alae*) which rode smallish ponies and used four-pronged saddles without stirrups. Stirrups seem to have been introduced from the east by the hard-riding Huns after *Britannia*'s time.

By the fourth century, things had changed. Usurpations and frequent changes of emperor led to something of a siege mentality in which the emperor's personal army was increased dramatically in size. Overall numbers dwindled too, although there is fierce debate on exactly by how much. Under Diocletian, the elite notion of Roman citizenship disappeared and increasingly Germanic and Danubian tribes were brought into the army on a paid basis as *foederati*. The old distinction between the regular legionaries and the *auxilia* broke down, so that both fought and were equipped in the same way. Professional soldiers expected payment, either in cash or land and trust collapsed when this did not happen. The Cyprian plague which raged for over twenty years in the third century was probably smallpox and it wiped out between 15 and 30 per cent of the entire empire. The army was particularly badly hit and never fully recovered. Added to this, from that period on and particularly in the time of *Britannia*, barbarian tribes were constantly invading, putting huge pressure on an army that saw an increase in desertions. It is not easy to compare the fighting efficiency of the fourth century soldier with his counterpart in the Principate. Informed writers like Ammianus Marcellinus (320-390), himself a soldier, saw no decline. Vegetius, writing in the late fourth century, was not a military man and believed he was wrong. Vegetius' military manual was still being read and followed in the fifteenth century.

Shields from the Notitia Dignitatum, *a list of Roman units c420.*

Top row (l to r): Honoriani Attacotti Seniores (the Attacotti tribe enlisted in the Roman army); Exculcatores Iuniores Britanniciani (the British Squashers!); Invicti Iuniores Britanniciani (Undefeated British)

Middle (I to r): Seguntienses (the ex-garrison of Segontium in North Wales; Secunda Britannia (formed from the old II Augusta Legion).

Bottom: Praesidienses (probably a unit of the XX Valeria Victrix Legion from Eboracum).

Organisations in the West

The Eastern provinces developed their armies in a different way and do not feature in the *Britannia* series. In the West, there were three types of army group:

a) *Comitatus Praesentalis* – the imperial escort, with headquarters at Mediolanum (Milan) who followed the emperor on campaign. The most elite of these were the *Scholae*, the cavalry unit.

b) *Comitatus* – the field armies, stationed in the diocese or group of provinces. Both a) and b) were mobile, increasingly reliant on cavalry to cover large distances.

c) *Exercitus Limitanei* – border troops such as those who guarded **Hadrian's Wall**. The assumption that these men were inferior to those of the field armies is not borne out by evidence.

Our information on the army of the fourth century comes largely from the *Notitia Dignitatum* (see HOW DO WE KNOW?) which lists various units, including barbarian *foederati* and even shows the designs of various shields. The book is not wholly accurate, but it is almost the only source we have.

Unit sizes varied and the figures are sketchy but most legions in the comitatus were 1000 strong, sub-divided into *vexillationes* of 500. *Limitanei* outfits might have been smaller still.

Joining the Eagles

Recruits for all types of unit were typically 20-25 years old when they enlisted, but men of 35 would not be turned down. They had to be physically fit – a legionary was expected to be able to march twenty miles a day carrying his armour, weapons and personal kit (*impedimenta*) and be able to build a makeshift camp before nightfall. In 367, the year of the Great Conspiracy, the minimum height requirement was reduced to five Roman feet and three palms (5ft 7in). The recruit was branded or tattooed on the arm (which helped identification if he deserted) and was given an ID tag which he wore around his neck as soldiers still do. He was also given a certificate (*probatoria*) and was then sent to a unit. His length of service was between 20 and 24 years. Leave could only be granted by a senior officer, a *dux*, *comes* or even *magister militum*.

The Cavalry (Ala)

Mounted units have always seen themselves as superior. Infantrymen do not see it like that! Horses were smaller than today, usually thirteen hands high and of a wide variety of local breeds. Saddles had four prongs to hold the rider firm and in the *Britannia* era, stirrups were unknown in the west. The cavalry carried lances (*conti*), long swords (*spathae*) and oval or circular shields. They were used as scouts and foragers on campaign and as shock troops on the battlefield. Usually, in battle formation, they formed the wings of an army. Mounted archers were common.

The Infantry (Legiones, Auxilia)

Traditionally the backbone of the Roman army, the footsoldiers had a fearsome reputation. Their training was tough and relentless. On the battlefield they marched in formation, shields interlocked, in silence. Only at the charge, when they were running at full tilt, would they roar out the *barritus*, the battle cry they had picked up from various enemies. Their spears were thrown or used to stab and when they were dispensed with, the spathae came into play. Daggers seem to have dropped out of use in fourth century battles.

The Artillery (Ballistae)

Any field army would have siege engines with it, although this was declining by the fourth century. Ballistae fired missiles, either into troop formations or to smash timber and stone fortifications. The most common type was the wild ass (*onager*) firing stones between ten and sixty-one pounds in weight. The range would vary, but about 180 paces would be needed for accuracy – perhaps 480 against a stationary target. The shooting rate would also vary; two shots a minute would be the norm.

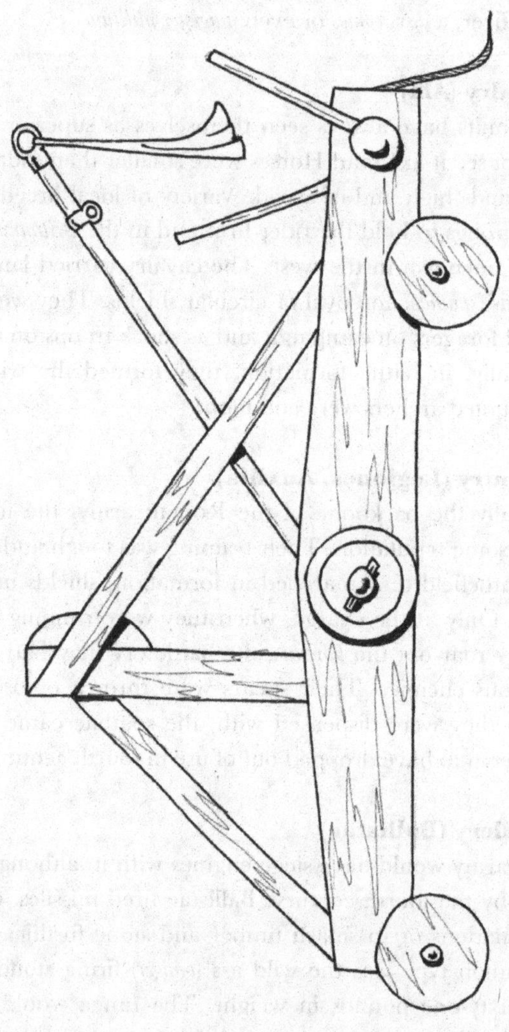

The Onager (or wild ass) as a stone throwing machine. The largest fired stone shot designed to smash fortifications. Smaller versions could be used against troop formations in the field.

Camps and Quarters

At the end of every day's march, a field army was expected to build a defensive camp, a ditch and earth rampart surmounted by stakes carried by the troops themselves. The larger and more elaborate of these became permanent legionary bases, like those at **Eboracum** (York) or **Deva** (Chester). They were traditionally rectangular, with rounded corners, like a playing card and were intersected with two straight roads. Near the centre would be the *principia*, the commander's quarters with officers' quarters nearby. Barracks, stables and workshops would be built inside the ramparts and there would usually be a parade ground and temple (*aedes*) where the legionary standards were kept. These – the silver eagle being the best known symbol – had a sacred quality about them, exactly as regimental colours still have in modern army units.

Men lived in the barracks in *contuberniae*, groups of eight (sometimes ten) and they were not expected to marry. In fact, marriage had originally been banned for Other Ranks by Augustus. Every permanent camp would have its *canabae*, however, a civilian town of camp followers. There were brothels here, *tabernae* (pubs), perhaps an amphitheatre and baths.

It was unusual for men to live 'under canvas' for long. The canvas was in fact leather, stretched over wooden frames and most squaddies complained bitterly about them.

Weapons and Equipment

The appearance of a fourth century soldier would have been very different from our traditional image, reinforced by Hollywood. At battles like Strasbourg in 357 it must have been difficult to tell friend from foe. All units wore a variant of the intercisa helmet or spangelhelm, an iron bowl of two sections with a central ridge, nasal and cheek plates. Both types gave good protection, but hearing was reduced and vision limited. While officers continued to wear the fancy, muscled cuirasses (breastplates) of the Principate, the rank and file wore mail or scale armour, down to the knee, over a woolen, long-sleeved

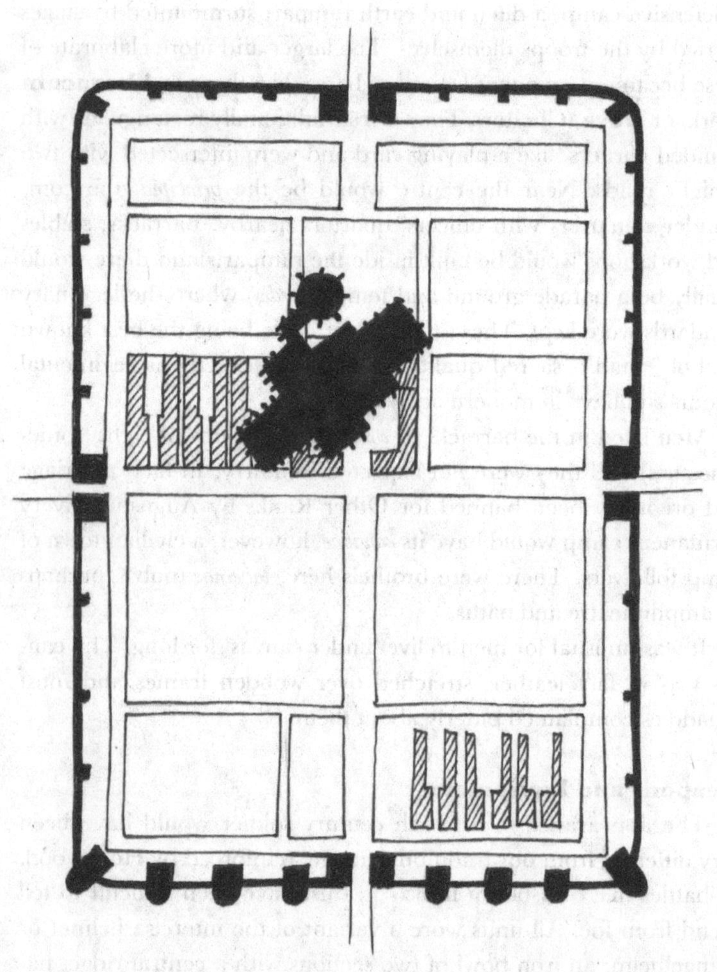

The huge fortress of the VI Victrix Legion at Eboracum.(York). The black shape in the centre is York Minster. The sheer scale of the fort can be measured by the fact that the Minster is 160m long.

A far cry from Hollywood – using all available evidence, a soldier of the Britannia period would have appeared on campaign like this.

tunic. In colder climates like Britannia, loose trousers laced at the ankle were the norm, as was a cloak, usually fastened with a brooch at the shoulder. All troops now used the cavalry *spatha*, up to three feet long, with a double-edged blade that could be used for slashing and thrusting. Shields were of wood with iron rims covered in raw-hide and, clipped behind them, the infantry carried darts (*plumbatiae*), which could be deadly at close quarters. Spears included the older *pilum* (javelin) for throwing, but more common were the conventional designs for stabbing and keeping the enemy at a distance. Footwear consisted of leather boots (*calcei*), hob-nailed for grip and laced over the front of the foot. Archers carried curved bows of yew or similar flexible wood and fired arrows carried in a quiver, from the chest. Specialist troops like slingers wore identical dress to everyone else. Their slings were leather and the shot were small, circular stones. Examples have been found with lettering on them, usually an offensive jibe at the enemy. Recent archaeological finds in Scotland have unearthed hollow shot that was probably designed to make a whistling roar as they hurtled through the air at up to 100mph, adding yet more terror to the battlefield.

The argument still rages as to how far the 'barbarianisation' of the Roman army led to its downfall. Most experts now believe that it did not; barbarians had been recruited as far back as Augustus' reign (27BC-14AD) and the increased use of *foederati* and leaders such as **Alaric** in no way reduced the efficiency of the fighting man by the time of *Britannia*.

The Legions of Britannia

The structure and organisation of the Roman army in the time of the *Britannia* period is very complex. The old style numbered legions were constantly merged and reshuffled. For simplicity's sake, we have taken the artistic license of referring to the units by their older names; but it is not outside the realms of possibility that units did not have a loyalty or knowledge of their 'parent' legions.

There were three legions stationed in the country during the *Britannia* period. They were the last to leave.

II Augusta

The Legio Secunda Augusta was created by the first emperor, Augustus and in 25BC was ordered to Hispania Tarraconensis (Spain). It stayed there until the disastrous defeat of the XVII, XVIII and XIX legions in the Teutoberg Forest in 9AD, when it was transferred to Mogontiacum (Mainz). After 17, it moved its headquarters to Argentoratum (Strasbourg) where tombstones (*stele*) of the unit have been discovered.

In 43 when Aulus Plautius invaded Britannia, the II were commanded by Titus Flavius Vespianus, the future emperor Vespasian. The legion captured thirty hill forts of the Durotriges and Dumnonii in the south as well as Vectis, the Isle of Wight. It lost to Caratacus and his fierce Silures warriors in 52 and suffered a degree of shame because of the hesitancy of its camp prefect Poenius Postumus, in the legion's response to Boudicca's rebellion in 60. He had orders from general Gaius Paulinus Suetonius to join him on the march to rout the rebel queen and he refused, perhaps preferring to defend Exeter against what might have become a more general uprising. When he realised his position, he fell on his sword and the legion marched without him.

In the following years, the II moved several times, to **Gleva** (Gloucester), **Isca Augusta** (Caerleon) and **Abonae** (Sea Mills, Bristol). In 122, the legion, along with others, built **Hadrian's Wall**, so central to the *Britannia* series and twenty years later, the **Antonine Wall**. There is an inscription to Julius Marcellinus, a centurion of the II, at **Banna** (Birdoswald). By the fourth century, the legion had moved to **Rutupiae** (Richborough) and it is listed in the *Notitia Dignitatum*. Its personal standard was the sea-goat or Capricorn, the birth sign of the emperor Augustus.

VI Victrix

Another legion raised under Augustus was the Legio Sexta Victrix, the 'victorious sixth'. It is first recorded in Perusia, today's Perugia, in 41BC and fought in the naval battle of Actium against Marcus Antonius (Mark Antony) and Cleopatra. Between 29 and 19BC the

VI served in Hispania (Spain) and earned the nickname Hispaniensis ('the Spanish'). Its headquarters was Léon, originally Legio, the legion's base and it also had units at Caesaraugusta (Zaragoza). The VI had a political reputation, backing its commander, Servinius Sulpicius Galba, against the hugely unpopular emperor Nero in 68.

In 119, the emperor Hadrian ordered the VI to Britannia, replacing the battle-depleted IX Hispana at **Eboracum** (York). Three years later, they were building their emperor's Wall alongside the **II Augusta** and the **Antonine Wall** after that. An influx of Sarmatians, warriors from today's Black Sea region, strengthened the VI on the orders of the emperor Marcus Aurelius, typical of the resettlement of *foederati* throughout the period. The legion obtained the nickname 'Fidelis Constans', faithful and loyal, which may refer to a campaign against northern tribes in the late second century. Under the emperor Septimus Severus, the VI invaded Scotland and was given the title 'Britannica', the British. At **Eboracum** in 306, the VI proclaimed Constantine emperor. **Stilicho** probably withdrew the last of the legion in 402, but it is possible that some kind of skeleton staff stayed on. The legion's personal emblem was the bull.

XX Valeria Victrix

The XX was yet another Augustan creation, dating from 31BC. The origin of Valeria is uncertain, but it may refer to its campaigns in Illyria (today's Croatia) under Marcus Valerius Messala, where it showed its mettle against superior numbers. After General Varro's defeat at the Teutoberg forest, the Valeria Victrix was sent to Oppidum Ubiorum (Cologne) and by 43 was among the units invading Britannia under Aulus Plautius. It defeated Caratacus at Caer Caradoc (perhaps a battlefield near Caersws) and seems then to have split, some cohorts going to **Camulodunum** (Colchester), others to **Gleva**

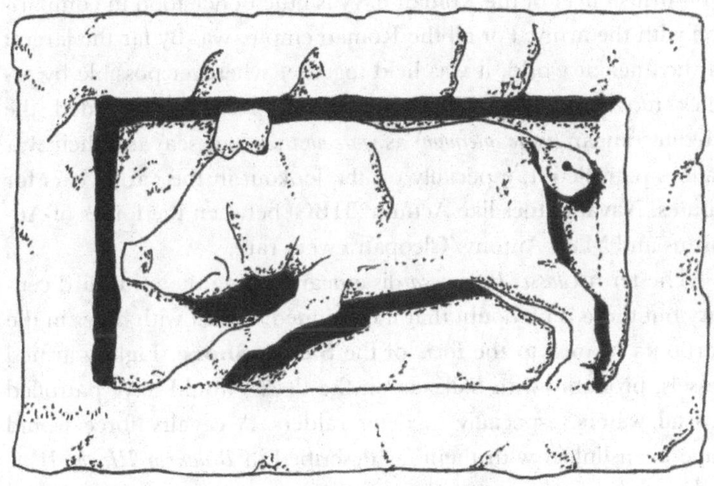

The standard of the XX Valeria Victrix legion from a building at Carrawburgh. The boar was a Celtic totemic animal too, believed to possess almost magical strength and ferocity.

(Gloucester) and **Viroconium Cornoviorum** (Wroxeter). During the Boudiccan revolt of 60-61, the **XX** defeated the Ordovices in central Wales and destroyed the Druids' altars on **Mona** (Anglesey).

Under Agricola in the campaigns in Scotland in 78-84, the legion was back south four years later, based permanently at **Deva** (Chester) but hired itself out to build **Hadrian's** and the **Antonine Wall**. After its backing of the usurper Carausius at the end of the third century, there is very little information on the **XX**. It fought on the Danube in 255 although this was probably a vexillation, not the entire legion. It is likely that the **XX** was taken from Britain by the usurper **Constantine** but no hard evidence exists. The legion's standard was the wild boar.

The Navy – Classis Britannica

The British fleet of the Roman navy is little understood in comparison with the army. For all the Roman empire was by far the largest in the ancient world, it was held together wherever possible by armies moving overland. That said, the Romans regarded the Mediterranean (*mare internum*) as *mare nostrum* (our sea) and their war galleys patrolled it, especially on the lookout in the early years for pirates. Naval battles like Actium (31BC) between the forces of Augustus and Mark Antony/Cleopatra were rare.

The term *Classis Britannica* disappears during the mid-third century but there is no doubt that it continued to exist with bases in the harbours nearest to the forts of the **Saxon Shore**. Lightly armed vessels, probably with ballistae on the decks, would have patrolled coastal waters, especially to deter raiders. A cavalry force would have been linked with them (as described in *Britannia III: the Warlords*).

The ships themselves remained the galleys of the Mediterranean, despite the generally heavier seas of the Channel (the German Sea) using the power combination of a single sail and oars.

Because information on the fleet is scant, its role in the *Britannia* series has been kept to a minimum.

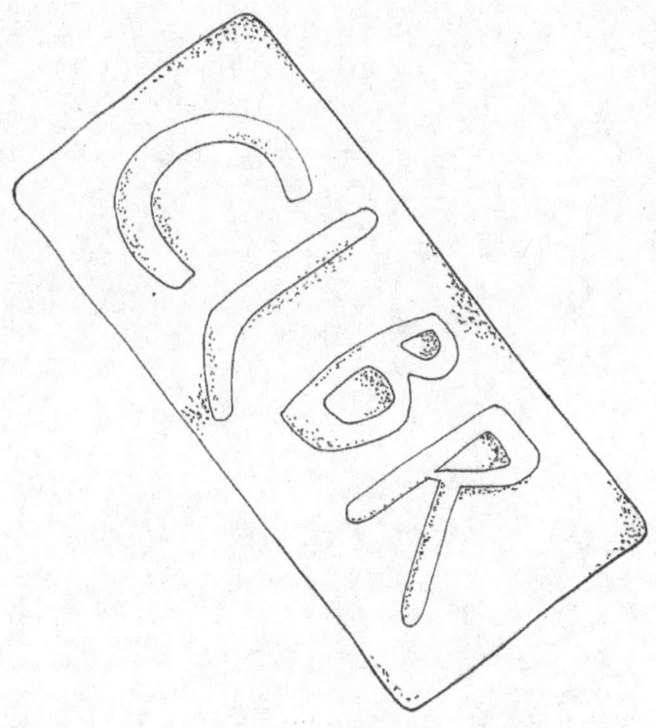

A tile from Beauport Park, East Sussex. The initials CLBR refer to Classis Britannica – the British fleet. Today, Beauport Park is a holiday centre but in the third century it was the third largest iron works in the Roman Empire. This tile probably came from a bath house.

THE ENEMY

THE ENEMY

'There also came the legion set to guard the furthest Britons, the legion that curbs the savage Scot and scans the lifeless patterns tattooed on the dying Picts.'

Claudian *The Gothic War*

As Rome expanded, it made enemies. Most of these were defeated, not once but many times and some of them became part of the empire and were absorbed into the army. Here we have a look at the opponents who appear in *Britannia* at a time when Rome's star was falling.

The Picts

The Romans called these natives of today's Scotland *picti*, the painted ones because of their habit of using blue-tinted woad to decorate their bodies for battle. Julius Caesar records this as early as 54BC and as far south as Sussex, so it had presumably once been a common Celtic practice. Because the Picts, like the Celts, had no written language, we have to rely on scant archaeological evidence or the Roman take on them. Cassius Dio (155-235) called them the *Caledonii* – Scotland generally was Caledonia – and they lived in 'wild and waterless mountains and desolate and swampy plains and possess neither walls, cities nor tilled fields, but live on their flocks, wild game and certain fruits … They dwell in tents, naked and unshod, possess their women in common … and they are very fond of plundering.'

Dio had never been to Scotland but he probably got his information from those who had. The country was indeed wild and desolate, but hardly waterless. Certainly the Picts were shepherds and cowherds rather than tillers of the soil, but they did grow crops in the Lowlands and their 'cities' were stone towers called brochs around which settlements grew up. Stone reliefs of their warriors show cavalry, spearmen and archers, lightly armed with virtually no armour. They raided habitually, attacking Lowland tribes like the **Votadini/Gododdin** and the Wall itself in the Great Conspiracy of 367. Their speed across rough terrain was impressive and they could vanish into the Highland fogs before a Roman unit could find them.

The Scots

The Scotti came, confusingly, from Ireland and we do not hear about them before the time of *Britannia* in the 360s. According to tenth century documentation, they came into Argyll from Ulster about 500BC but like most later evidence, this is debatable. They spoke a Q-Celtic form of Gaelic (see **WHO SPOKE WHAT**) and we cannot assume, despite the Great Conspiracy, that they had much in common with either the Picts or the Irish with whom they marched that summer.

The Scots fought like all barbarians, charging (in their case almost entirely on foot) in wild disorder, leaping and yelling to rattle the Roman opposition. They threw themselves onto the legionaries' shields, hacking with their swords and stabbing with their spears, but they lacked the cohesion of Roman troops and were invariably routed.

Settling in Pictish lands and establishing a rapport with them led to the creation of the clan system, an extension of the tribal original.

The Hiberni

Because the Scotti came from Ireland, there is considerable confusion between the two groups. They are often lumped together as Scots-Irish but actually spent more time fighting each other than banding together. We know they used their sea-going curraghs (coracles) to raid the coast of Wales and the West Country, perhaps as far east as Hampshire and the Isle of Wight. Like the much later Vikings, they could hit the coast anywhere, destroy a village and sail away again, before any attack could be mounted against them.

As far as is known, there was never a serious attempt to launch a Roman invasion of Ireland although one general believed he could do it with two legions and auxiliaries. One of the problems in researching Hiberni history is that it is hopelessly bound up with Gaelic legend and facts tend to vanish into the mists of magic. They called themselves Goidel or Eriu.

The Attacotti

This tribal group of marauders is among the most shadowy and enigmatic of *Britannia's* enemies. They turn up in Ammianus Marcellinus' account of the Great Conspiracy and because they are lumped with the Picts, Irish and Scots, the assumption is usually made that they came from roughly the same area, perhaps the Western Isles. There is also some suggestion that they originated in Northern Europe, however, possibly Norway.

The hermit and future saint Jerome describes them in various writings, claiming that the Attacotti held their women and children in common and did not marry in the conventional way. Jerome claims to have seen the Attacotti in Gaul as a young man and that they delighted, during their sheep and cattle raids, in cutting off the buttocks and breasts of shepherds and shepherdesses. He says they ate human flesh, although this is a common claim by 'civilised' writers against anyone they considered to be barbarians.

They are listed in *Notitia Dignitatum* as being part of the Roman army strength, but not in Britain. We know it was common practice to incorporate beaten enemies as *foederati*, so that makes some sense. The Attacotti Honoriari Iuniores was stationed in Italy, its senior unit and the Attacotti Iunieres Gallicoii, in Gaul. Presumably, they had curbed their eating excesses by then!

The Saxons

The traditional view in Old School history books is that the Angles,

Saxons and Jutes, from North Germany and southern Denmark, invaded Britannia after the legions left and pushed the Romano-British natives to Wales and the West Country, despite a heroic stand by that great Celtic myth, Arthur. We now know that the arrival of the Saxons was infinitely more complicated than that and more insidious. The fact that the east coast of what is now England was referred to in the late fourth century as the **Saxon Shore** may describe a situation in which there were already Saxon settlements there. In terms of archaeology, we start to find clear evidence of these settlements from the 430s, *after* the *Britannia* period, but the name 'Saxones' appears in the Latin written record in the third century. It was a catch-all term, like *Germani* or *barbari* to mean any foreigner from beyond the northern limits of the empire.

There were economic reasons for the Saxons to move west, but such movements were going on among barbarians generally, scenting perhaps that Rome's days were numbered. The problem is that all the chroniclers of the early Saxon period – Bede, Gildas, Nennius for example – lived years later and their accounts either deal with a later period or make errors of judgement about the *Britannia* era.

It is safe to say that Saxons had been raiding the east coast of Britannia for years by 367 and were considered enough of a problem for the Saxon shore forts to be strengthened at that time.

A Pictish warrior. The exact design of the tattoos on the skin are unknown. The cloak is a forerunner of modern tartan and was essential for the weather conditions north of Hadrian's Wall.

WHO SPOKE WHAT

WHO SPOKE WHAT

One of the most intractable problems in studying history is trying to imagine how our ancestors *sounded*. Auditory experience is one of the most important of all. We can tell moods, from happiness to hatred via irony and a hundred other points of view by the inflection in a single word. We know what Shakespeare's characters say on stage, but is that how Elizabethans spoke to each other over the morning's manchet bread or while waiting for the play to start? We simply do not know. Thanks to the miracles of Victorian technology, we can still hear the voices of Florence Nightingale, Charles Dickens and William Gladstone. But the voices of Theodosius the Great, Magnus Maximus, Stilicho? Nothing. Instead, we only have the written word. Except that the Celts and most of Rome's enemies had no written language at the time of *Britannia* so we only have a partial picture anyway.

The Romans spoke Latin and because of the sheer size of the empire, an educated native of Cornwall could, in theory, converse with his or her counterpart three and a half thousand miles away in Iraq. We must, of course, stress *educated* because it was largely the upper classes, the landowners, politicians and businessmen who used the *lingua Latina*. Conventionally, the verb in Latin is at the end of sentences and there are, as older readers might remember, strict rules that struck terror into the hearts of generations of schoolchildren. Nominative, vocative, accusative, genitive, dative, ablative were words carved into our flesh – the different endings of Latin nouns. Verbs had a horror of their own – past, present, future, perfect, pluperfect, etcetera, etcetera (that's Latin too) and we do not believe for a moment that the average Roman was any better at learning all this than most of us today at grappling with English grammar. Proof lies in the graffiti scratched on walls from Ratae Coritanorum (Leicester) to Pompeii – it is rough linguistically and much of it is untranslatable in a family book!

Because the Romans had occupied Britannia for four hundred years by the time of the series, it is highly likely that many of the locals had picked up the rudiments of Latin, especially those who dealt regularly with army camps, towns, officials. Likewise, it is at least probable that the 'Romans' learned a smattering of the local Celtic dialect, especially when it came to *limitanei* troops who married into native families. Their children were probably functionally bilingual even if they wrote nothing down; or, if they did, they wrote in Latin. A little under half modern English words have a Latin origin – their counterparts can be found in France, Spain, Italy and elsewhere.

The Romans used a system called *tria nomina* (three names) until well after the *Britannia* period. The *praenomen* was a personal name, chosen by a child's parents, traditionally given to a son on the ninth day of his life and a daughter on the eighth. This was usually a family name, of one of the parents, another relative or an ancestor. Next came the *nomen*, the family name which explained status and pedigree. By the time of *Britannia*, these distinctions were less important than they had been in the old days of the Republic. The *cognomen* was another personal name, often a physical description or a nickname, usually earned and given by others. So, Caius Julius Caesar, probably the most famous Roman of them all, was actually Caius of the Julian family. Caesar was an ironic nickname for a man with a receding hairline – it meant hairy! One of the oddities about the Roman use of language is that while the senior emperor under the tetrarchy was Augustus – the wise – his second in command was Caesar – the hairy.

The natives of Britannia continued to speak their own Celtic language throughout the Roman occupation. So, peasants on a villa estate or tin miners for example would have spoken Celtic to each other, but understood orders in Latin from their bosses and could reply in the same language.

The Celts used a highly complex language system that had two broad developments. The first, used in Ireland, was the Goidelic form which would have been spoken in *Britannia* by **Niall Mugmedon of the Nine Hostages** and his warriors. The other type, obviously more widespread in the series, is the Brythonic form. Both these terms were coined by linguists in the nineteenth century. After the seminal work by scholar Kenneth H. Jackson in 1953 – *Language and History in Early Britain* – Brythonic became Brittonic and there are two variants of it – P Celtic and Q Celtic. Brittonic would have been spoken all over what is today England and migrated to Armorica, today's Brittany, perhaps because **Magnus Maximus** took so many troops and camp followers with him in 383. Goidelic was spoken in modern Ireland and south western Scotland; the rest of Scotland would have had its own Pictish tongue.

Some Celtic words have survived to the present day or nearly so. The sheep-counting yan, tan, tethera became one, two, three. Peat, dad, noggin, gob and hubbub are other examples.

HOW DO WE KNOW?

HOW DO WE KNOW?

What are the historical sources for *Britannia*? They are listed below but, first, a word of caution. The study of History as a discipline did not emerge until the nineteenth century and things we now take for granted, like the weighing of probabilities and in-depth analysis of evidence, did not exist before that. The men discussed here were chroniclers, for the most part polymaths who were fascinated by everything in the world and tried to write it all down. They rarely had first-hand experience, relying instead on hearsay, myth and legend; and they often wrote years after the events or people they were writing about. All of their work must be taken with a pinch of salt (see COFFEE WITH DIOCLETIAN). We have deliberately not included scholars like Nennius, Gildas and Bede because they belong to a much later generation and have a moralistic, Christian take on the events they wrote about.

Ammianus Marcellinus *Res Gestae*

Marcellinus, most probably from Antioch in Syria, was a Greek-speaking soldier who wrote *Res Gestae* in Rome after his retirement. The work covers the period from the emperor Nerva (96) to the battle of Adrianople (378) and the death of Valens. He fought under Constantine II and Julian in Gaul and Persia and his military knowledge makes him an important critic of events. He was probably pagan but takes no side in the recurring acts of sectarian violence during his lifetime – 'no wild beasts are so deadly to humans as most Christians are to each other.'

Only eighteen of a possible thirty-six books have survived, covering the later period 353-378. As ever, the problem is that the oldest surviving copy we have dates from the ninth century and there are several gaps in the text.

Because Marcellinus knew Julian he is full of praise for him, referring to the emperor's inability to cross to Britain in 360 because he was heavily committed militarily in Gaul. He describes the Great Conspiracy in one line – 'The Picts and Saxons and Scots and Attacotti harassed the Britons with continual afflictions', but the term for the event – 'barbarica conspiratio' – comes from him.

Antonine Itinerary – *Itinerarium Antonini Augusti*

This is a unique list of settlements in Roman Britain and describes various routes – fifteen journeys in all – around the country. The name comes from an association with Antoninus Pius, the second century emperor linked with the wall in today's Scotland. The oldest known copy dates from the time of Diocletian (late third century) but the original source may have been an official survey carried out under Augustus. It may have been intended for government officials and/or the army and not all the place names can be identified. (See FRAGMENTI ET ROBERTI for Roman distances)

Claudius Claudianus

A Greek poet probably born in 370, Claudius effectively became laureate at the court of the emperor **Honorius** in Mediolanum (Milan). He wrote panegyrics on the great men of his day, especially **Stilicho.** The Senate voted a statue to him in Rome in 400 and **Stilicho**'s wife, **Serena**, found Claudius a rich widow to marry.

Notitia Dignitatum

This 'list of offices' is vital for an understanding of the army during the *Britannia* period. It covers the whole empire with details of army units, equipment, camps and cities, even the designs on legionary shields. Court officials, military commanders and governors are listed. The section dealing with the West probably dates from around 420, by which time some of the units listed had already left Britannia (so the information must have been collated earlier). There are many gaps in the record and units are sometimes listed twice under the different commands. The problem is that the *Notitia* may have been incorrect to begin with, but additional errors have crept in up to the fifteenth century, which is the date of the actual manuscript that has survived.

Orosius *Historiarium Adversum Paganos*

The seven books of Orosius' work form an important record of pagan people and events in the early years of Christianity. Paulus Orosius was born around 375, possibly in Bracara Augusta (Braga today) in Hispania. He travelled widely and knew luminaries of the Christian church like Augustine of Hippo and Jerome. In terms of historical methodology, Orosius is unusually clear, admitting his Christian bias that since the coming of Christ, the world is a better place. He says little about Britannia, however, dismissing **Magnus Maximus** in a single line – 'an energetic man … and honourable and worthy of the throne had he not arrived at it by usurpation contrary to his oath of allegiance …' He is equally contemptuous of the other usurpers – 'while [the Alans, Suebi and Vandals] were running wild over the Gauls, in Britain **Gratian**, a citizen of the island, was made a usurper and was killed. In his place, **Constantine**, a man of the lowest military rank, on account of the hope alone which came from his name and without any merit or courage, was elected.' After 407, Orosius is silent.

Ptolemy *Geographia*

Ptolemy was a Greek philosopher living in the second century and working in Alexandria, Egypt. The *Geographia* is his second great work and Christopher Columbus was still using it to plot his voyage of 1492. A fifteenth century copy of Ptolemy's map of Britannia (it is not known whether he actually ever drew one himself) is recognizable in terms of coastline, although today's Scotland is at right angles to what would become England. Even so, his placing of various tribal regions seems to be largely correct.

Vegetius *De Re Militari*

Publius Flavius Vegetius Renatius was not a soldier and probably not a vet, although his two works are on the army (*De Re Militari*) and veterinary medicine (*Digesta Artis Mulomedicinae*).

We know nothing about the man beyond the scant information he gives in his books, but the last event referred to in *De Re Militari* is the death of the emperor **Gratian** in 383. Vegetius was a Christian and his work is dedicated to the emperor **Theodosius**, although this dedication may have been made later. His description of recruitment, training, tactics, camps and so on was treated as gospel by later generations, his maxims still being implemented by the Prussian Frederick the Great in the eighteenth century. Vegetius believed that the army of his day (late fourth century) was a shadow of its former self under the Principate and his bias may have misled historians for centuries.

Zosimus *Historia Nova*

Zosimus' New History was compiled at the turn of the fifth/sixth centuries and deals with the period from the reign of Augustus to the early fifth century, shortly before **Alaric**'s sack of Rome in 410. A Greek living in Byzantium, he was probably a government official reaching the rank of count (*comes*) and most of his writings are anti-Christian.

Book VI of the *Historia* deals with Britannia, a country he never visited and the events he describes took place a century before he wrote. It is particularly chaotic in style. From him comes the reference to the famous Rescript of **Honorius**, the official document which effectively told Britannia it was on its own and could expect no help from him. It is unclear whether this was genuine or whether it referred to another part of the empire that had asked for help. Zosimus places all the blame on the usurper **Constantine.**

Archaeology

The Romans were such innovators and worked on such a grand scale that we have been left with a surprising amount of evidence in the physical landscape today. Crucially, unlike their iron age predecessors and Saxon and Angle successors, they built in stone, not wood, which does not degrade like the timber used by other cultures. The Romans were so good at building that much of their civic development, particularly in Britain, was carried over by subsequent generations, whether it was the layout of a town and its defences or through the reuse of building materials. But there is also a vast amount of evidence in the ground and that can only be properly analysed and assessed through excavation and survey.

Excavations have led to the discovery of villas such as the one at Fishbourne in West Sussex, which was in a back garden, to the discovery of a burnt bed in Colchester, associated with the Iceni queen Boudicca razing it to the ground. It is worth noting that although there is evidence in the archaeological record of London, St Albans and Colchester to attest to the burning of sites contemporaneous with Boudicca, none of the thousands she is supposed to have killed according to Roman historians have ever been found. She was a victim of character assassination perhaps and also a salutary lesson that we should use all the source material and up-to-date evidence possible.

The idea of digging up the past is not new, but it has developed immeasurably over the course of the last century from enthusiastic amateurs with inexact techniques and poor recording methods to world-renowned professionals using electromagnetic pulses and complex carbon-dating technology.

One very early technique still employed today is aerial photography and survey. After its application for the military, one of the first uses of the aeroplane was in fact by archaeologists. Being able to view and record a site from the air gives a complete picture of how a town or fortress was laid out and perhaps suggests why, based on the surrounding landscape. Additionally, aerial photography can be used to identify sites that are not visible at ground level. Sites which lie beneath the ground can be evidenced from discoloration to topsoil, and from the air, these are even clearer as circular or rectilinear marks in the landscape. Today, technology has come on to the extent that aerial photographers can now employ lidar, a technique which allows detailed 3D mapping of the ground to create not only tangible landscapes but also detect anomalies in the ground that cannot be seen with the naked eye.

Another technique that helps identify potential archaeological features without having to break out spade and mattock is resistivity surveying or geophysics. The use of a resistivity meter can help plot the extent, depth and dimensions of a site and its buildings. Simply put, electromagnetic impulses fired into the ground return information as they come into contact with more solid objects. This can mean walls and foundations but it can also be naturally occurring obstructions, so careful analysis of the information is crucial. Even so, this this technique can be invaluable in assessing sites which cannot be excavated further for a variety of reasons.

Other techniques used to establish a time-frame such as dendrochronology, dating associated wood samples from artefacts or felled timber to establish a *terminus post quem* (date after which) or Carbon14 dating, which can give very wide chronologies are undoubtedly a huge resource, but are perhaps not as necessary in the dating of Roman Britain, and this is due to the literate nature of the Romans. Minted coins have dates on them and even simply the depiction of leaders on these coins can lead to an educated guess as to their chronology. The Romans were also very keen on memorialising the dead, so epitaphs and memorials are common and also give us an insight into how they viewed the afterlife.

There are sometimes tensions in carrying out archaeological digs. All too often, finds are made by accident when a new building project is being undertaken. Delays while research goes on cost money and, in the centre of a town or city, cause chaos. Frequently, archaeology is a matter of rescue, working against the clock. It was on that basis that the television series *Time Team* set up their essentially artificial three-day digs.

FRAGMENTI ET ROBERTI!

FRAGMENTI ET ROBERTI!

Bits and Bobs!

Inevitably, in the *Britannia* series, there are a number of facets of Romano-British life that are mentioned, often without explanation (see COFFEE WITH DIOCLETIAN). Some of these are detailed below.

Slaves

Pre-Roman Celts already had a slave economy to an extent. Defeated enemies became prisoners of war who became slaves. This was always a risky business; in the first century BC there were three successive slave revolts against Rome, the last one led by the gladiator Spartacus. Most of the participants were former warriors and were used to violence as a way of life. But for most of the time, the slaves of the *latifundia* (field hands) were third or fourth generation who accepted their lot in life and gave little trouble.

Slaves came in all shapes and sizes, from well-educated Greeks who advised emperors to condemned men (*noxii*) sentenced to the metal mines, lead in Northumberland, tin in Cornwall and gold in Wales. They were bought and sold as any other commodity, the most expensive being young women because of their child-bearing potential. Little children and the old would often be thrown in as a job lot. They worked at whatever task their owners gave them and, like the black slaves of America in the nineteenth century, close bonds were often formed between slave and master. In times of stress, they could be used as pawns. In 406, when the emperor **Honorius** was letting the Western provinces drift, he suggested offering freedom to slaves to join the provinces' defence.

Slaves could marry and often, like the free poor, formed burial clubs to ensure a plot of land for themselves and their families. A slave could be flogged and even beaten to death on the whim of his master in the early years, although women and children could not.

We have no accurate numbers of slaves but they outnumbered free citizens considerably. One figure for the first century BC tells of a ratio of 4:1 in Rome itself. There was always an edginess about this, especially in the overcrowded towns, but on a rural villa estate, the problem was the same – more of 'them' than of 'us'. By the time of *Britannia*, Stoic philosophy and Christianity were combining to give a more humane outlook in slave-master relationships. Legislation from Augustus onwards led to ever greater protection for slaves. Manumission was common; the setting free of slaves, for example, on the death of a master. Traditionally, for a single day during the midwinter Saturnalia, all slaves were free; this was the origin of Twelfth Night, when the Lord of Misrule held sway. More permanently, many men left orders for manumission of their slaves in their wills.

Such increased understanding counted for little when the chips were down. When **Alaric** attacked Rome in 410, thousands of slaves streamed out of the city to join him.

Jews

We have no accurate information on Jewish communities in Britannia. In the series, we have a pogrom carried out by Gratian in Augusta Treverorum (Trier) which is in keeping with the increasingly harsh official attitudes to Jews from the third century onwards. The pattern of repression was a microcosm of what the world would see again in the centuries ahead. Anti-Jewish propaganda was followed by persecution and eventually segregation in ghettoes. Under Constantinus in the 330s, Jews could not own Christian slaves. If a Jewish slave owner circumcised a slave, that would merit the death penalty. No Jew could marry a Gentile. It is interesting that the only relaxation of this persecution occurred under the emperor Julian, called the Apostate by the Christians because he tried to re-establish the traditional gods and values of old Rome. He planned to let Jews resettle Jerusalem and to rebuild the temple destroyed by Vespasian in 70. On his death, anti-Semitism continued.

Medicine

Our word 'doctor' meant a trainer to the Romans, as in a man who trains gladiators. Doctors to the Romans were *medici* and they all subscribed to the views of the most celebrated physician of his day, Claudius Galen (c. 130-200) whose ideas were still being followed until the scientific revolution of the seventeenth century. He wrote extensively and synthesised the medical knowledge of the Greeks, especially the four humours.

Aristotle wrote that the human body is 'composed out of the Warm, the Cold, the Dry and the Moist' (Galen's synthesis). All diseases were seen in relation to this and such was the intellectual power of Greek philosophy that no one in the *Britannia* era seems to have challenged it. That said, there was a more modern take on disease from Aulus Cornelius Celsus in the first century AD who wrote, 'Diseases were [in ancient times] ascribed to the anger of the immortal gods and from them help used to be sought.' It was indolence and luxury, Celsus believed, that actually caused disease and we are not that far from this notion of two millennia ago to tobacco, alcohol and over-eating today!

There was a whole range of home-spun remedies, some sanctioned by physicians, others not, which would have been used in Britannia as they were in other parts of the empire. In his *Natural History*, Pliny deals with 'illnesses' like toothache, ulcers, animal bites, dropsy, leprosy, epilepsy and insanity. While complaining bitterly about quack medicines and charm pedlars, Pliny admits that superstitious people queue up to use both. For snake bites, the saliva of a fasting person was good, especially if the spitting occurred three times. It was pretty useful against epilepsy too and could even be handy in protecting someone against witchcraft. Of course, if you were to meet a person lame in the right leg, you were on your own! The crushed jawbone of a pig knitted broken bones effectively, as did boiled lungs, although for broken ribs, there was nothing better than goat's dung and a little old wine. Fevers were a problem. Venison was useful, so was the salted right eye of a wolf. A mixture of cat's dung and the toe of an owl could prevent a relapse.

It is easy to laugh at Roman 'medicine' and it quickly becomes something out of the witches on the heath in *Macbeth*. It is only when we read Pliny's urging of the use of goat's milk and honey that we begin to realise that homeopathy has its place and that perhaps the Romans knew a thing or two, after all!

Food and Drink

Archaeological evidence has filled out the record of how Romano-Britons kept body and soul together. Work carried out at **Calleva Atrebatum** (Silchester) has revealed venison, hare and boar as common meats. All three animals were routinely hunted in the *Britannia* period, as much for sport as for food. Fish at Silchester included pike and perch which would have been plentiful in the country's rivers and lakes but herring, smoked or dried, was the most common. The salt which had once been part of a soldier's pay (*salarium*) was mined in areas like Cheshire and was used as a preservative. Seafood was popular, mussel, cockle and oyster shells having been found in abundance. Honey provided sweetness in the centuries before refined sugar. Columella and other writers on agriculture have useful tips on bee-keeping and it may be that villas had their own hives for this purpose. Fruits like apples and pears were plentiful too, with orchards on the villa estates and the edges of towns.

Other foodstuffs had to be imported, (as we saw in TOWN ...) Olive oil and garum (fish sauce) were transported in amphorae stored in sand in the holds of merchant ships. Most food seems to have been heavily spiced, perhaps to disguise the rather 'old' produce available in the shops; the Romans did not do 'sell by dates'!

Wine was imported too, although, as we have seen, there were vineyards in Britannia. Traditionally, at least according to Roman writers, the Celts were obsessed with the stuff. Diodorus Siculus (90-30BC) wrote that they drank it unmixed, implying that the Romans watered theirs, which made them stupidly drunk very quickly. They even suggest that a primary reason for Celtic invasions of Italy was to gain access to the vineyards there. All of this, of course, is a racial slur. The Celts drank ale or beer which was considered barbaric, although they also drank mead, a honeyed wine which the Romans enjoyed too.

Roman wine came in four types – black, red, white and yellow and there were much-prized vintages for the true wine-lover: *Caecuban*, *seitan* and *falernian* were the most sought after. Villa wine cellars have yielded glass jars sealed with gypsum and labelled with the date that the contents were laid down. *Calda* was mulled wine, drunk warm, especially in the winter. *Posca* was rot-gut stuff, little better than vinegar, traditionally drunk by soldiers and slaves.

Most Romans ate three meals a day. *Jentaculum* was breakfast, taken soon after sunrise. Sometimes it might be just a little water, but more usually comprised wheat pancakes, bread in wine, cheese, honey, dried fruits, dates and olives. *Prandium* was our lunch, eaten at the sixth hour. Eggs, bread and cheese were popular then. *Cena* was dinner, but at the ninth or tenth hour was often eaten in the afternoon. This could be a wheatmeal porridge and fish, but it was often the main meal of the day. Historians have rightly been fascinated by the excess of lavish Roman meals, especially in the Principate and early Empire, with stories of gold plates and jewelled cutlery, stuffed swans, larks' tongues and barbecued dormice. It is worth reminding ourselves that most Romans, especially in the provinces, *never* ate like that, any more than most of us do today. Meat was usually boiled rather than roasted. Bread was the most common food, made in flat circular loaves of wheatflour or bran. *Frumentum* was popular too – corn made into porridge.

Clothes, Hair and Beauty

Our over-riding image of Rome is the toga, a *huge* rectangle of linen around the bodies of politicians hurrying to the Senate to assassinate Julius Caesar on the Ides of March in 44BC! By the time of *Britannia*, the toga was ancient history and altogether more comfortable and practical clothing had replaced it.

Men

From the skin out, a male civilian of the *Britannia* period wore underpants (*subigaculum*) of linen or wool which tied at the waist. Shirts were unknown but the body was covered with a tunic, long-sleeved and tightly-fitting, usually made of wool and embroidered or dyed. A second tunic might be worn over this in colder weather, but for serious winters, a fur cloak and hood was essential. These garments were prized by Romans, perhaps because they were a novelty. Most cloaks were fastened at the shoulder with a bronze pin or brooch. Leggings were a cross between tights and trousers, usually fastened at the ankles with ties. Sandals might still be worn in the summer months but the more robust *calceus* (boot) had replaced the open-work *caligae* for soldiers.

The problem with accuracy regarding dress is that most depictions come from statues and *stele* of important − and often fabulously rich − individuals and we cannot be sure they are shown wearing everyday dress. A statue of Honorius from Barletta in the years soon after *Britannia* shows the emperor with the forward-combed hair worn by every emperor in honour of Julius Caesar, a muscled cuirass that had not changed for five hundred years, a linen, much-folded cloak and knee-high boots. **Stilicho**, from about 400 on a carved panel in Monza Cathedral shows the same hairstyle, a beard and a cloak and tunic. His spear and sword are of the type carried by all legionaries and auxiliaries.

Women

From the skin out, Romano-British ladies wore an undergarment not unlike a modern petticoat. There are examples of leather bikinis, but these were almost certainly for gymnastic wear. The outer garments were variants of the earlier tunica, palla and stola, with draped cloth caught up by brooches. A Roman matron usually wore her hair piled high, often adorned with jewellery. Only children and young girls wore their hair loose.

Jewellery, often imported from Gaul, Germania or Britannia (jet) was widely worn by rich women, comprising a tiara or diadem, brooches, rings and necklaces, made of gold or silver. Some of this, at least, had a ritual significance – a snake, for example, symbolized fertility.

Hairstyles were infinitely varied and wealthy women often had slaves, whose only job was to use goat tallow and beech ash to dye or tint the mistress' locks. The hair of captives, especially Germanic blondes, was especially prized for wigs. Powder and rouge were widely used for the skin. White brought out the complexion. Blue emphasized the veins. Black was essential as eye-liner.

As with all matters that cost money, the poorer elements of society had to make do and mend rather than replace garments as they wore out. To be able to spin and weave wool and craft leather were essential skills of the working class, traditionally carried out in the long winter weeks when the fields were idle.

High class woman and child wearing the clothes shown on gravestones and in graves themselves from the time of Britannia.

Weights and measures

For anyone who has lived through Imperial and Metric and still can't remember how many centimetres there are in an inch (or even if it is that way around!) the Roman weights and measures bring no comfort. There are slight variations throughout the history of the Roman Republic and Empire in weights and measures and some scholarly disagreement, but for what it is worth, here are some of the problems which would have troubled the average Roman.

Distance

Uncia - Roman inch (very close to modern inch or 2.4cm)
Pes - 12 unciae (inches) (1 foot or 29cm)
Passus - 5 pedes (feet) (4.8ft or 1.48m)
Actus - 120 pedes (feet) (116ft 6in or 35.5m)
Mille Passus - 1000 passus (1 Roman mile or 1.48km)

Weight

Uncia - Roman ounce (1 ounce or 28g)
Libra - Roman pound, 12 unciae (3/4 pound or 328g)

Area

Pes Quadratus - (square foot or 0.9m2)
Jugerum - (5/8 acre or 2530 square ft)
Heredium - 2 Jugera (1.246 acres or 5060 square ft)
Centuria - 100 heredia (124.6 acres or 50.5 hectares)

Volume

Ligula (spoonful) (1.14cl)
Hemina - .273ltr
Congius - 12 Heminae (3.22ltr)
Amphora - 8 congii (25.79ltr)

Money

The economics of the late Roman empire was chaotic and would take a whole book to explain fully. The main things upon which the empire's economy were based are easy to remember – the four Ts; trade, taxation, troops and territory. Payment for troops in particular was a thorny subject and often didn't happen at all, or was goods in kind rather than money. For those crippled by the punitive taxes levied by the crumbling empire its final fall was probably a huge relief! The coinage was as follows, with a solidus as the largest unit.

1 Solidus = 12 Miliarense = 24 Siliqua = 180 Follis = 7,200 Numma.

A pocketful of small change would have been quite a challenge to carry about!

Time

Roman days were 24 hours long, with 12 hours in the day and 12 hours in the night divided into four 'watches'. A Roman minute was in fact 24 of our minutes and a Roman second was 24 seconds.

Days

In English, we name our days of the week after Germanic Polytheistic Gods from the conquering Anglo-Saxons (except Saturday, and possibly Monday and Sunday) unlike the Romance languages.

Dies Lunae: Monday (Luna's day) [Moon's Day]

Dies Martis: Tuesday (Mars' day) [Tiw - God of War]

Dies Mercurii: Wednesday (Mercury's day) [Woden - Principal God]

Dies Jovis: Thursday (Jupiter's day) [Thunor - God of Thunder]

Dies Veneris: Friday (Venus' day) [Frigg - wife of Woden]

Dies Saturni: Saturday (Saturn's day) [Saturn's day]

Dies Solis: Sunday (Sol's day) [Sun's day]

Weeks

There were several variations of recording a week. Whereas the Jewish/Christian Sabbath was Saturday, the week we recognise today comes from Constantine the Great who made Dies Solis the day of rest, in honour of the God Sol Invictus, the Unconquered Sun.

Months
Martius: March (Mars' month)
Aprilis: April (Month of openings)
Maius: May (Maia's month)
Junius: June (Juno's month)
Julius: July (formerly Quintilis, renamed in honour of Julius Caesar)
Augustus: August (formerly Sextilis, renamed in honour of Augustus Caesar)
Septembris: September (seven)
Octobris: October (eight)
Novembris: November (nine)
Decembris: December (ten)
Januarius: January (Janus' month)
Februarius: February (Month of purification)

Years
The Romans had a complicated way of measuring years involving who was consul of the Empire at the time. The modern system of Before Christ (BC) and Anno Domini/Year of the Lord (AD) was not conceived until the sixth century. In modern times it is generally referred to as Common Era and Before Common Era.

COFFEE WITH DIOCLETIAN

COFFEE WITH DIOCLETIAN

During the writing of the *Britannia* trilogy, one of us went on holiday to Croatia (the Roman Dalmatia) and had a cup of coffee in Split, a beautiful town on the tourist trail. The old town was the emperor Diocletian's retirement palace and modern shops, bars and homes are built into the second century walls. This is by way of explaining the title of this chapter; Diocletian does not appear in *Britannia* and Europe would have to wait fourteen hundred years before anybody actually sat down to drink coffee. To us, the phrase said it all. The task of the novelist is very different from that of the historian. Fiction is not fact. How do you marry the two, to produce what some people call 'faction'?

If you have read thus far in this book you will have seen 'possibly', 'probably', 'perhaps' without number. We do not apologize for this – they are the stock words of the historian. To begin with, there are colossal gaps in our knowledge. As Rome lost its grip on the empire, the written record was consigned to the flames. The recording of events lost its importance and future generations like ours have to live with that. As we have seen, archaeology has come to the rescue, but no geophysics in the world is going to give us the colour of Magnus Maximus' eyes or the length of Elen Luyddog's hair. Even when we have that rarity, incontrovertible proof of a past event, historians have an annoying habit of arguing among themselves over its exact meaning and interpretation.

For the novelist, what this adds up to is both a blessing and a curse. It is a curse because we do not have the full picture; there are just some questions we cannot answer. It is a blessing because that very lack of knowledge gives the novelist carte blanche to use his/her imagination. And to tell a story, we have to do just that; we have to make hundreds of judgement calls per novel. Did Stilicho *really* ever come to Britannia? We do not know, but saying we do not makes for a pretty limp story. He either did or he didn't. We decided he did. Did he preside over an attack on the temple of Isis in Londinium? There is no record of that; but this does not mean it did not happen, merely that no one thought to write it down. Similarly, we had to make a judgement call on exactly where Valentia was and we placed it north of Hadrian's Wall.

There are reviewers who nitpick about such matters. We have got this wrong or that happened five years later than we say. That particular event took place in *that* city, not *that* one. In our combined historical experience of nearly eighty years, neither of us has ever read an historical novel or seen an historical film which has *ever* got it right. That is not because of the lack of information mentioned above but because in telling an exciting story, a writer has to follow rules. The story cannot be *too* complicated or the reader will lose interest. There have to be 'goodies' and 'baddies' because that is how fiction works. There has to be love interest and there has to be blood and guts, to appeal to all tastes.

We believe strongly that 'plonking' is wrong. A 'plonk' is historical writers' slang for an obvious point driven home with a sledgehammer, e.g. 'Don't forget, Julius Caesar, to wear your second-best toga when you go to the Capitol today, the Ides of March, 44BC, in case anyone should stab you in the back or anything.' This kind of writing may help the reader with not much background knowledge, but it does become very irritating, very quickly.

All this must occur within a plausible historical framework but occasionally writers feel obliged to step outside the box. So Manda Scott in her excellent fiction series on Boudicca has the future queen of the Iceni killing her first man at twelve. There is nothing in the historical record to tell us that she personally ever killed any-one; but it makes her an edgier, more gripping character. Likewise, Simon Scarrow, perhaps the best known 'Roman' writer today, has his soldiers screaming, 'Incoming arrows' during a battle. 'Incoming' is first recorded of shells in the Vietnam War; but we understand the drama of the situation and it works.

For the sake of dramatic licence, we twisted the legend of St Patrick. According to one account, he was sixteen when he was captured by pirates, but in the fourth century, a sixteen-year-old was a man. We thought it much more gripping to have Patrick a little boy. We cheated enormously with people's ages to make the action in *Britannia* fast and exciting. Given Justinus' age at the start of *The Wall*, he would be at least eighty-one at the end of *The War-lords*! *Mea culpa* as the Romans would have said.

It bothered us that we allowed four 'squaddies' from the Wall to gain elevated status throughout the *Britannia* series. To not spoil the story for anyone reading *World of Britannia* before the trilogy, I will not go into further detail, but suffice to say none of it is remotely likely, but at the same time, the relatively humble Constantine III *did* stake a claim to the emperor's throne in 407 and for a time did very well against enormous odds. The end of Rome was a time of chaos, the ordered world turned upside down. And in that context, all bets are off and characters can behave as they like.

We have enormously enjoyed writing the *Britannia* trilogy and this accompanying book. And if they have encouraged you to dip your calceus into the murky waters of Roman Britain just a *little* deeper, then our job is done.

Ave atque Vale, lectore!

PLACES TO VIS-IT

We are very fortunate in Britain that great organisations such as English Heritage among many others, take such pride and care in our history and very few Roman sites are neglected. This list is not exhaustive but briefly highlights a few of our favourite sites which are all well worth a visit. Website links correct at time of publication.

England (North-East)

Aesica Roman Fort, Northumberland
http://explore-hadrians-wall.com/roman-sites/great_chesters
Though little remains of Aesica, it is a pleasant walk and has an altar stone where people continue to offer their loose change to the gods.

Aldborough, North Yorkshire
http://www.english-heritage.org.uk/visit/places/aldborough-roman-site/
Aldborough contains two excellent Roman mosaics, a museum and a section of the original town wall.

Arbeia Roman Fort, Northumberland
https://arbeiaromanfort.org.uk/

This impressive site features a reconstructed barracks, gatehouse and a museum and is often host to various events and fun days.

Binchester Roman Fort, County Durham

http://www.durham.gov.uk/binchester

Binchester Fort includes the impressive remains of a bath house and commander's house.

Carrawburgh, Northumberland

http://www.english-heritage.org.uk/visit/places/temple-of-mithras-carrawburgh-hadrians-wall/

Though the three altars of Carrawburgh are replicas, this little gem is a must-see for those in the area. The original altars are housed in the Museum of Antiquities in Newcastle.

Cilurnum, Nothumberland

http://www.english-heritage.org.uk/visit/places/chesters-roman-fort-and-museum-hadrians-wall/

The most complete Roman cavalry fort in Britain is complemented by a museum, tea-room and a host of family activities throughout the year.

Hadrian's Wall

http://hadrianswallcountry.co.uk/

Hadrian's Wall is too expansive to list in too much detail but there are countless attractions and sites along it.

Housesteads, Northumberland

http://www.english-heritage.org.uk/visit/places/housesteads-roman-fort-hadrians-wall/

This excellent site along Hadrian's Wall includes a museum and visitor centre.

Vindolanda, Northumberland

http://www.vindolanda.com/

Vindolanda is a must-see and perhaps the best experience for those interested in Hadrian's Wall. The site is remarkable and reconstructed forts, an interactive museum and the Vindolanda tablets really bring Roman Britain to life.

Eboracum (York), North Yorkshire

http://www.yorkshiremuseum.org.uk/exhibition/eboracum-roman-festival-2016/

The picturesque city of York is extremely proud of its Roman heritage and with good reason. With Roman remains underneath York Minster, a great museum and countless Roman finds dotted throughout, it is a must-see – and all watched over by the modern statue of Constantine the Great.

England (North-West)

Birdoswald Roman Fort, Cumbria

http://www.english-heritage.org.uk/visit/places/birdoswald-roman-fort-hadrians-wall/

A picturesque walk, exhibition, tea room and the longest continuous stretch of Hadrian's Wall.

Hadrian's Wall

http://hadrianswallcountry.co.uk/

Hadrian's Wall is too expansive to list in too much detail but there are countless attractions and sites along it.

Chester Roman Amphitheatre, Cheshire

http://www.english-heritage.org.uk/visit/places/chester-roman-amphitheatre/

The remains of Britain's largest amphitheatre are enjoyed by the locals to this day.

England (South-East)

Bignor Roman Villa, Sussex

http://www.bignorromanvilla.co.uk/

The remains of Bignor Roman villa include an excellent mosaic (and a farm for the children).

Brading Roman Villa, Isle of Wight

http://www.bradingromanvilla.org.uk/

This elegant villa has excellent mosaics, interactive exhibits, a wonderful view over the sea – and a very good coffee shop.

Burgh Castle, Suffolk

http://www.english-heritage.org.uk/visit/places/burgh-castle/

The impressive stone walls of this Saxon Shore fort remain and rest in beautiful countryside, making it well worth a visit.

Calleva Atrebatum, Hampshire

http://www.english-heritage.org.uk/visit/places/silchester-roman-city-walls-and-amphitheatre/

The city walls of this stunning site near Silchester still survive and make for a beautiful walk. The nearby remains of the amphitheatre can also be visited and archaeological digs open to the public often take place.

Camulodunum, Essex

http://www.visitcolchester.com/visitor-info/Roman-Colchester.aspx

Although eventually overshadowed by London in importance, Roman Colchester is still very impressive, including the oldest church and the only known circus. As well as several museums there is also the Balkerne Gate, Britain's largest surviving gateway.

Dubris, Kent
http://www.dovermuseum.co.uk/Home.aspx
The Roman lighthouse still proudly stands alongside St. Mary's church in Dover and the Roman Painted House is also well worth a visit.

Fishbourne Roman Palace, West Sussex
http://www.visitchichester.org/activity/fishbourne-roman-palace-and-gardens
The largest known Roman residence north of the Alps is a fantastic day out for all. The breath-taking mosaics and recreated Roman garden make this one of Roman Britain's best.

Lullingstone Roman Villa, Kent
http://www.english-heritage.org.uk/visit/places/lullingstone-roman-villa/
Another outstanding Roman villa complimented by a light-show and costumes for the kids.

London Wall, London
http://www.english-heritage.org.uk/visit/places/london-wall/
This section of the Roman wall at Tower Hill has survived very well and is accompanied by a statue of the emperor Trajan.

Noveum Museum & Roman Baths, Chichester
http://www.thenovium.org/
This museum is home to the remains of a Roman bath house amongst its impressive collection.

Pevensey Roman Fort, East Sussex
http://www.english-heritage.org.uk/visit/places/pevensey-castle/
The remains of this impressive Saxon shore fort are still imposing to this day.

Portchester Roman Fort, Hampshire
http://www.english-heritage.org.uk/visit/places/portchester-

castle/
Arguably the best preserved Saxon shore fort in Britain. This is a must see for fans of Roman history.

Richborough Castle, Kent
http://www.english-heritage.org.uk/visit/places/richborough-roman-fort-and-amphitheatre/
Monumental at both the beginning and end of Roman Britain, the Saxon Shore fort of Rutupiae and its museum is well worth a visit and a boat trip to the castle from Sandwich is a highlight.

Temple of Mithras, London
http://www.historic-uk.com/HistoryMagazine/DestinationsUK/The-Temple-of-Mithras/
Thanks to Bloomberg and the Museum of London, the Temple of Mithras still stands proudly among modern Londinium.

Verulamium, St Albans, Hertfordshire
http://www.stalbansmuseums.org.uk/verulamium/
The Verulamium Museum houses an impressive collection from St Albans' Roman past.

Winchester City Walls, Hampshire
http://www.visitwinchester.co.uk/
Although little remains of Venta Belgarum, the historic city of Winchester is well worth a visit.

Welwyn Roman Baths, Hertfordshire
http://www.hertfordshiremuseums.org.uk/museum.php?id=31
The remains of Welwyn's Roman Baths are well cared for after some brilliant rescue archaeology work in the 1970s.

England (South-West)

Chedworth Roman Villa, Gloucestershire

http://www.nationaltrust.org.uk/chedworth-roman-villa
A museum and picnic area complement the beautiful mosaics discovered in one of the biggest villas in the country.

Exeter City Wall, Devon

http://www.exploredevon.info/activities/geology/exeter-city-walls-cathedral/
Sadly, much of old Exeter was flattened in the Baedecker raids in 1942-3, but the ghost of the Roman town still remains.

Littlecote Roman Villa, Wiltshire

https://historicengland.org.uk/advice/heritage-at-risk/search-register/list-entry/1255269
Littlecote is a Roman villa with pagan connections and The Orpheus Mosaic remains is one of the most well-known in the country.

Lunt Fort, Baginton, Warwickshire

http://www.luntromanfort.org/
Lunt Fort contains a partially reconstructed wooden fort and gyrus, used for cavalry training.

Roman Baths, Bath

http://www.romanbaths.co.uk/
One of Roman Britain's most famous and lively sites. The popular Roman Baths and its collections are a must see set within the beautiful town of Bath and can be combined with a relaxing spa in a more modern setting.

Viroconium Cornoviorum (Wroxeter), Shropshire

http://www.english-heritage.org.uk/visit/places/wroxeter-roman-city/
With the largest free standing Roman ruin in Britain, an excellent museum and reconstructed town house, Wroxeter is highly recommended.

Scotland

Antonine Wall
www.antoninewall.org
The Antonine Wall runs the width of Scotland between the Firth of Forth and the Firth of Clyde. Some of the most impressive sites include Rough Castle, the Hunterian Museum and Bearsden.

Inchtuthil, Perthshire
http://www.castlesfortsbattles.co.uk/perth_fife/inchtuthil_roman_fort.html
Although only earthworks and a field remain, it is still worth a visit and one of the most northerly Roman forts.

Castlecary, North Lanarkshire
http://www.antoninewall.org/visiting-the-wall/things-to-see-and-do/site-by-site/castlecary
The remains of this fort of the Antonine Wall make an excellent addition to any walk or bike ride.

Wales

Caer Gybi, Anglesey
http://cadw.gov.wales/daysout/caer-gybi-roman-fortlet/?lang=en
A small Roman fort with the walls still in good condition

Caerleon (Isca Augusta), Gwent
http://www.visitwales.com/things-to-do/attractions/museums-galleries/museums/national-roman-legion-museum
Caerleon is a must-see for those interested in Roman Britain. As well as the remains of the amphitheatre there are sections of the wall and barrack buildings. The town itself includes the impressive National Roman Legion Museum and the Roman Baths Museum.

Cardiff Roman Fort, Cardiff
http://www.britainexpress.com/attractions.htm?attraction=811

Cardiff Castle itself is a great day out and has been built over the old Roman fort but sections of the Wall and a reconstructed gateway can be visited.

Dolaucothi Gold Mines, Carmarthenshire

http://www.nationaltrust.org.uk/dolaucothi-gold-mines

An excellent family day out with guided tours.

Segontium, Gwynedd

http://www.nationaltrust.org.uk/segontium

Another pleasant day out to visit the remains of the Roman fort.

Venta Silurum, Monmouthshire

http://cadw.gov.wales/daysout/caerwent-roman-town/?lang=en

Arguably the best surviving Roman town walls in Britain, standing 5m and the remains of the basilica, forum and temple can be visited at Caerwent.

GLOSSARY

Ala(e)	Cavalry in the Roman Army
Alans	Nomadic tribe from central Asia – barbarians
Alemanni	Germanic tribe – barbarians
Annona	Roman goddess associated with corn, similar to Ceres. Also the term used for the ration payments issued to soldiers from local levies
Aquilifer	Legionary who carried the Aquila, the legion's eagle standard
Atargatis	Fertility goddess worshipped by the Romans, but of Syrian origin
Attacotti	Marauding tribe known for their viciousness. It is uncertain where they came from - barbarians
Badb	Celtic war goddess, usually found in the shape of a crow
Baestasians	Germanic tribe – barbarians
Ballista	Missiles and weapons of the Roman army
Belatucadros	Sun and war god worshipped by the Votadini/Gododdin
Biarchus	Roman official responsible for provisions
Calceus	Roman army boot which replaced the laced caligae sandals in the third century

Cena	Mid-afternoon or evening meal
Cerberus	Many-headed dog that guards the gates of the underworld
Circitor	Sergeant in the Roman army
Civitas	City, usually in the provinces
Chi-Rho	Symbol and monogram of Christ
Comes Litoris Saxonici	Count of the Saxon Shore
Comitatenses	Mobile field soldiers
Consul	Highest elected official in the Roman administration
Contubernium	Squad of eight (sometimes ten) Roman soldiers
Contus	Cavalry lance
Cornicen	Roman army horn player
Cornu	Roman army battle horn (bugle)
Curia	Court or assembly (see ordo)
Danaan	Faerie race of Irish folklore
Deceangli	Celtic tribe of North Wales
Decurion	Civil or military official, usually a member of the aristocracy
Denarius	Coin (traditionally one penny)
Diocese	Group of provinces e.g. Britannia
Donativum	Cash handed out to Roman soldiers on the accession of a new Emperor
Draco	Dragon standard
Draconarius	Dragon standard-bearer
Dux Britanniarum	Military commander of Britannia
Farum	Lighthouse (from the Greek *pharos*)
Flagrum	Whip, cat of nine tails
Flidais	Celtic/Irish goddess of forests and the hunt; the Roman Diana
Foederati	Barbarian troops who fought for Rome in exchange for land, cash etc.
Franks	Germanic tribe – barbarians
Germani	Collective term for various peoples beyond the river Rhine barbarians
Gododdin	Celtic tribe living north of Hadrian's Wall

Goidel	Celtic term for the Irish
Goths	Germanic tribe – barbarians
Grannos	Celtic sun god associated with healing
Gustatio	'Starters', first course of a meal
Heruli	Germanic troops in the Roman army
Hiberni	Roman term for the Irish
Huns	Nomadic tribe from central Asia – barbarians
Hypocaust	Under-floor central heating system in Roman buildings
Ides	Middle of a month (13th or 15th day)
Imbolc	Celtic festival marking the beginning of spring
Isis	Egyptian goddess, worshipped in Britannia
Jentaculum	Breakfast
Jutes	Germanic tribe from Denmark – barbarians
Kalends	First day of each month in the Roman calendar
Laeti	Foreign tribes who were allowed to settle on Roman soil
Laigin	People and province of today's Leinster
Lancea	Spear
Libra	Roman unit of weight (approx. 340g)
Limes	Border defences of the Roman empire e.g. Hadrian's Wall
Limitanei	Border troops of the Roman army
Lorica	Armour, usually breastplate
Magister Equitum	Cavalry commander, Master of the Horse in the Roman army
Magister Militum	Commander in the Roman army, general
Magister Peditum	Infantry commander in Roman army
Mansio	Official inn/hotel for travellers
Medicus	Doctor (of medicine)
Miles	Soldier
Minerva	Roman goddess of wisdom
Mithraeum	Temple to Mithras
Necropolis	City of the dead, cemetery
Nemesis	Roman goddess of revenge

Nones   The ninth day before the Ides of a month
Oceanus   God of the Sea (Neptune)
Onager 'Wild ass', a catapult used by the Roman artillery
Optio   Junior officer (below centurion) in the Roman army
Orcus   Roman god of the underworld
Ordo   Council, court, local government
Ossipago   Roman household goddess responsible for the growth of a baby
Palastaula   Roman basilica or town hall
Palatini   Palace troops, the emperor's personal bodyguard
Pallium   Tunic worn by members of the nobility and clergy
Pedes   Infantryman
Plumbata   Military, weighted darts
Praeco   Town crier, herald
Praeses   Governor of part of a province, e.g. Britannia Secunda
Praetorian prefecture Largest administrative area of the Roman Empire, e.g. Gaul
Primus Pilus   Senior centurion of legion in the Roman army (first spear)
Principia   Headquarters of a legionary commander in a camp
Rivros   February to March in the Celtic calendar
Sacristan   Official in the Christian church
Saex   One-edged sword from which the Saxons took their name
Sagittarius   Archer in the Roman army
Sanctum   Sacred or holy place, shrine
Saturnalia   Roman religious festival, 17-23 December in honour of Saturn, god of farming
Saxons   Germanic tribe – barbarians
Scotti   Tribe from Ireland, settling in today's Scotland - barbarians
Schola Palatina   The emperor's cavalry bodyguard

Semisallis	Corporal in the Roman army
Signifer	Standard bearer in the Roman army
Sol Invictus	The Unconquered Sun, god worshipped especially by Roman soldiers
Solidus	Gold, high value coin
Spangenhelm	'Germanic' helmet increasingly worn by cavalry and officers
Spatha	Long-bladed sword carried in the Roman army
Spiculum	Javelin
Subligaculum	Underwear
Suebi	Germanic tribe – barbarians
Taranis	Celtic god of thunder
Tartarus	Roman underworld, Hell
Tellus Mater	Roman household goddess, Mother Earth
Turma	Cavalry squadron; subdivision of an Ala
Ulaid	Irish-Celtic tribe from Northern Ireland (Ulster)
Valetudinarium	Hospital
Vallum	Ditch and defensive earthworks
Vandals	Germanic tribe – barbarians
Vexillation	Unit of soldiers, sub-division of a legion
Vexillum	Military flag or standard
Vicarius	Governor of a diocese
Vicus	Civilian neighbourhood
Votadini	Roman name for the Gododdin
Vulcan	Roman god of fire

GLOSSARY OF PLACE-NAMES

Abona: Bristol
Aegyptus: Egypt
Aesica: Great Chesters, Northumberland
Anderitum: Pevensey Castle, East Sussex
Aquae Sulis: Bath, Gloucestershire
Aquileia: Italian city near Venice
Arbeia: Fort in South Shields, Tyne and Wear
Augusta Treverorum: Trier, Germany
Belgica: Tribal region that roughly covers modern Belgium
Boderia: Firth of Forth, Scotland
Bononia: Bologna, Italy
Branodunum: Saxon Shore Fort, Norfolk
Britannia Prima: One of five provinces of Britannia, covering Wales and south-west England
Britannia Secunda: One of five provinces of Britannia, covering north England
Caeseraugusta: Zaragoza, Spin
Carthago: Carthage, Tunisia
Cataractonium: Catterick
Clausentum: Bitterne, Hampshire
Clota: River Clyde

Constantinople: Istanbul, Turkey

Dal Riata: Irish Kingdom which ruled lands in Ireland and Scotland

Deva: Chester

Din Eidyn: Edinburgh

Din Paladyr: Traprain Law, Scotland

Dubris: Dover

Durnovaria: Dorchester

Eboracum: York

Flavia Caesariensis: One of five provinces of Britannia, covering central England

Gallia: Part of the Roman Empire that roughly covers modern France, Luxembourg and Belgium

German Sea: North Sea

Hadrianopolis: Edirne, Turkey

Hasta: Asti, Italy

Hebros: River Maritsa, Turkey

Hibernia: Ireland

Hibernian Sea: Irish Sea

Hierosolyma: Jerusalem

Icena: River Itchen

Isca Augusta: Caerleon

Isca Dumnoniorum: Exeter

Lindum: Lincoln

Llyn Tegid: Bala Lake, Wales

Maxima Caesariensis: One of five provinces of Britannia, covering south-east England

Mediolanum: Milan, Italy

Mona: Anglesey

Narbonensis: Province in Gaul

Natiso: River Natisone, Italy

Oceanus: Atlantic Ocean

Onnum: Halton Chesters, Northumberland

Pinnata Castra: Inchtuthil Fort, Perth and Kinross

Pollentia: Pollenso, Italy

Portus Adurni: Portchester Castle, Hampshire

Portus Leminis: Lympne Fort, Kent
Regulbium: Saxon Shore Fort, Kent
Rutupiae: Richborough Castle, Kent
Saxon Shore: Coastal defences from Norfolk to Hampshire
Sorviodunum: Old Sarum, Wiltshire
Tarraconesis: Roman province of Spain
Thamesis: River Thames
Tynus: River Tyne
Valentia: Short-lived fifth province of Britannia, perhaps north of Hadrian's Wall
Vectis: Isle of Wight
Venta: River Wensum
Verulamium: St Albans
Vienna: Vienne, France
Viroconium: Wroxeter
Vindolanda: Bardon Mill, Northumberland
Vindovala: Rudchester

GLOSSARY OF TERMS

Ala(e): Cavalry regiment(s)

Alans: Nomadic tribe

Alemanni: Germanic tribe

Aquilifer: Roman military eagle-standard bearer

Baestasians: Germanic tribe

Belatucadros: Celtic god of war

Cena: Mid-afternoon / evening meal

Circitor: Rank above semisallis in Roman army

Chi-Rho: Christian symbol and monogram

Comes Litoris Saxonici: Count of the Saxon Shore

Contubernium: Roman squad of eight (or ten) soldiers

Contus: Cavalry lance

Cornicen: Roman military horn player

Danaan: Faery race of Irish folklore

Deceangli: Celtic tribe of North Wales

Decurion: Member of the nobility

Donativum: Special payment to soldiers on the accession of a new emperor

Draconarius: Roman military dragon-standard bearer

Dux Britannorum (Britanniarum): Military general in Britain

Farum: Lighthouse

Flagrum: Cat-o'-nine-tails

Fustuarium: Cudgelling

Germani: Collective term to describe the various peoples beyond the river Rhine

Gododdin: Celtic tribe north of Hadrian's Wall

Goth: Germanic tribe

Gustatio: First course of a meal

Heruli: Germanic people serving in the Roman army

Hiberni: Roman term for the Irish

Imbolc: Celtic festival

Isis: Egyptian goddess

Jentaculum: Breakfast

Juti: Germanic tribe from Denmark

Lancea: Spear

Limitanei: Border soldiers

Lorica: Armour

Magister Militum: Commander of the Roman Army

Mansio: Official inn for travellers

Medicus / Medici: Doctor(s)

Necropolis: 'City of the dead', cemetery

Nemesis: Roman goddess of revenge

Optio: Rank below centurion in the Roman army

Ordo (curia): Council / court

Pedes / Pedites: Foot soldier(s)

Praeco(nes): Town crier(s)

Primus Pilus: 'First Spear', senior centurion of a legion

Sacristan: Role within the Roman Church

Scotti: Roman term for the Irish

Schola Palatina(e): Emperor's Bodyguard(s)

Semisallis: Rank above pedes in the Roman army

Signifer: Roman military standard bearer

Solidus: High-value Roman coin

Spangenhelm: Military helmet

Spatha: Sword carried by Roman army

Spiculum: Javelin

Subligaculum: Undergarment
Suebi: Germanic tribe
Tartarus: Roman underworld
Turma: Cavalry squadron
Valetudinarium: Hospital
Vallum: Defensive earthworks
Vandals: Germanic tribe
Vexillation: Detachment of soldiers
Vexillum: A military standard
Vicarius: Governor of a diocese
Votadini: Roman name for the Gododdin
Vulcan: Roman god of fire

MAP

BRITANNIA: Late 4th Century
Din Eidyn
Din Paladyr
VALENTIA
The Wall
BRITANNIA SECUNDA
THE GERMAN SEA
Eboracum
FLAVIA CAESARIENSIS
Segontium
Caer Llyn
Deva
BRITANNIA PRIMA
MAXIMA CAESARIENSIS
Londinium
THE SAXON SHORE

www.blkdogpublishing.com